YOUR JOB

SURVIVAL
OR
SATISFACTION
?

Jerry and Mary White

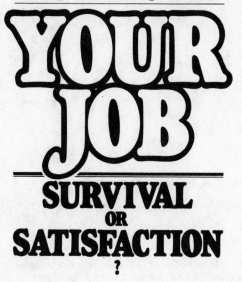

YOUR JOB

SURVIVAL
OR
SATISFACTION
?

Foreword by Lorne C. Sanny

ZONDERVAN
PUBLISHING HOUSE OF THE ZONDERVAN CORPORATION
GRAND RAPIDS, MICHIGAN 49506

YOUR JOB — SURVIVAL OR SATISFACTION?

Copyright © 1977 by The Zondervan Corporation

Unless otherwise indicated, Scripture quotations are from the
New American Standard Bible © The Lockman Foundation
1960, 1962, 1963, 1968, 1971, 1972.

Library of Congress Cataloging in Publication Data

White, Jerry E   1937 -
  Your job — survival or satisfaction?

  1. Work (Theology)   2. Job satisfaction.   3. Vocation.
I. White, Mary Ann, 1935 -   joint author.
II. Title.
BT738.5.W5   248'.88   76-45191

ISBN 0-310-34321-6

Printed in the United States of America

83 84 85 86 87 88 — 20 19 18 17 16 15 14 13

To
Robert Shepler

My first employer —
who taught me the satisfaction of
excellence in work
and
who influenced me
to become a Christian

CONTENTS

Work • Determining the Extent and Capacity of
Spiritual Gifts • The Challenge • Discussion Questions

Part II • CIRCUMSTANCES

FOREWORD

Whether your present occupation is a problem-free, happy situation or whether you struggle daily with moral and spiritual survival in your job environment — or your experience is somewhere between those extremes — you will find some profitable ideas in this timely book both to use and to pass on to others. No book I have read, Christian or secular, has these practical suggestions for people on the job, and all placed in a spiritual perspective.

And no wonder! Jerry and Mary White have had first-hand experience with a wide variety of situations — the academic world, space science and technology, working singles, homemakers, full-time Christian vocations, traveling. Their own Christian discipleship has been tested in many circumstances.

Out of their rich experience and their knowledge of scriptural principles, Jerry and Mary have produced a practical handbook for the working man and woman. They have winnowed out extremely helpful guidelines and suggestions from Scripture for the person working at a regular job or an unusual one, for everyone from salesman to assembly line worker, for the secretary or the homemaker, the "full-time Christian worker," and the government employee.

I commend this book to everyone who works for a living — and who doesn't? He should have it on his shelf for ready reference. It will be especially handy to use with those who come for counsel and advice about relating their jobs to the totality of their lives.

LORNE C. SANNY
President, The Navigators

INTRODUCTION

IT WAS 10:30 P.M. when the phone on my desk rang. My first reaction was irritation. It had been a long day of mind-stretching work and complex personal interaction. I was tired, and I was in the middle of a serious counseling session. Reluctantly I picked up the phone.

"Hello, Jerry. This is Brian Wilson."

A pang of embarrassment passed through me. I had neglected to return his call of just an hour ago. I sensed an emptiness in his voice that told me something was wrong. I made a lame apology for not returning his call.

"I'm being fired from my job," he said in an emotionally flat tone.

Knowing him, I was amazed. "Why?"

"For incompetence."

He had been confronted by his boss and was told his work did not meet even minimum standards. Expecting he would make excuses and tell me the reasons the boss was wrong, I asked, "Do you agree with him?"

"Yes, I do. I think I may be incompetent. Maybe I should quit now. Maybe I'm in the wrong line of work. In your seminar on work you mentioned this kind of situation. Can we get together to talk?"

Was God playing a bitter joke on Brian Wilson? He was twelve years into his career, held a master's degree, and had a good record to this point. Now it was all ruined — or was it?

Brian is different from many who speak to me about work only in that his frustrations and problems had reached crisis level. What about the security feelings of the salesman in that same seminar who was trying to figure out how to survive, using Christian principles in his dog-eat-dog business? Or the mechanic who countered the salesman's comments with his dilemma of "those of us common workers" trying to keep their jobs while competing with people who cheat on production and performance to make themselves look good.

Two years ago I was speaking to a group of single adults on living the Christian life in the real world. I casually included a brief session on their relationships to their jobs. A time bomb exploded! There were many questions, strong feelings of frustration, and a general sense of dissatisfaction with their success in integrating their jobs with their Christian lives. It was obvious that I had touched a sensitive nerve. The interest was so intense that I continued the discussion the next week. I tried to find resource material for them, but very little was available — especially for the nonmanager or nonexecutive, who punches a time clock and has little freedom to control his work or time.

I began to speak on the specific topic of work to other groups — students, couples, older workers, housewives, laboring and professionally trained people. The reaction was virtually the same — intense interest, underlying dissatisfaction, frustration, and uncertainty about the importance of work to the Christian. Yet many greatly enjoyed their work and had successfully integrated it into their lives. Their probing questions, the wise insights, and my personal experience and study of the Scriptures gave birth to this book.

The book has two parts. Part I (chapters 1 to 6) contains material foundational to all jobs. It must be read to give meaning and substance to part II. Part II (chapters 7 to 14) gives

practical suggestions for various classes and kinds of employment. The entire book is meant to be practical, not just
philosophical; it is meant to have clear biblical foundations.

I have personally struggled with the pressures of a secular
job, family needs, and personal ministry. The concepts taught
here are not just theory, but a result of my personal experience
and the counsel and input of others who have faced work
circumstances that I have not. The Navigators, with their
historical emphasis on servanthood and excellence in work,
have profoundly influenced my thinking.

I am greatly indebted to my wife, Mary, who diligently
edited and restructured my colloquial speech to readable
prose. She critiqued the contents from a woman's viewpoint
and is the author of chapters 9 and 10. It would be absurd for a
man to try to write about homemaking or careers for women!
Special appreciation is due my secretary, Mrs. Pru Zimmer,
for faithfully typing the various drafts of the book.

JERRY WHITE
Colorado Springs
April 1976

PART I

FOUNDATIONS

In your lifetime you will spend about 40 percent of your waking hours in your job. Will those hours be spent in frustration or fulfillment? This depends largely on how you fit your job into the totality of your life.

The basic issues of work, adverse circumstances, purpose in work and life, changing jobs, use of time, and ambition are discussed in part I. They are both foundational and practical. After building these foundations, you may read the particular chapters in part II that apply to you.

CHAPTER 1

THE BIBLICAL VIEW
OF WORK

Young MAN," he growled, "there's not another man in this factory who can turn out a part to exact specs like I can. I can do it faster — and better. Watch this!" He grabbed a piece of steel from a bin and mounted it on the lathe. He deftly made adjustments on the machine. Within seconds he hit the switch, and the starting growl of the motor gave way to a whine that drowned out his explanation of each step in the process. Even though I couldn't hear him, I could see a mixed pride and concern as he began shaping and turning the metal. After several machines, piles of steel shavings, special checks with a smudged set of drawings, and a final dip in cold water, he handed me the finished product.

"What do you think of that?" he beamed.

"It's amazing!" I said as I turned the warm metal in my hand. He meant the part, but I meant that his attitude was amazing. He *really* enjoyed his work.

"What about him?" I asked as I pointed to a young man in his early twenties standing about fifteen feet away. "Could he do this?"

14

"Nope," he said.

"Why not?"

"Well, first off, he doesn't care. Second, he won't take time to learn how to do it right. But mostly he just doesn't like to work. You can't do anything right if you don't like what you're doing."

As I walked away I reflected that this man was genuinely happy. That is unusual — especially rare is a man who is happy in his job and in life. Multitudes of others merely tolerate and endure their work as a means of getting money to buy food and feed the family to regain strength to be able to go to work again.

As I discuss this dilemma with people, I find that few are completely satisfied with their jobs and few know where it should fit with the rest of their lives. Personal conflicts, over-work, overambition, financial pressure, fear of unemploy-ment, boredom, lack of opportunity, and countless other prob-lems plague their existence. Some like work too much and neglect the family; others hate work and dread every day; some ignore the problems and go through the day like robots.

Engineers, machinists, housewives, secretaries, drafts-men, lawyers, salesmen, assembly line workers, and managers — regardless of the job, the frustrations remain the same. Many spend their lives trying to escape from the stark reality of pouring 25 percent of their lifetime into a job they hate. We give the majority of our adult lives to our work, but too often with the job comes conflict. The work is either too difficult or too boring. It is too demanding or offers no chal-lenge. The pay may be poor or if the salary is adequate, the work takes too much time. The work is mediocre, but the alternative is unemployment.

It is even worse if you are a Christian and are *supposed* to enjoy life and not have the problems and concerns common to the world. That is good theory, but in reality it is obvious that Christians also have fears, unpaid bills, overextended charge accounts, conflicts on the job, consuming ambition to get ahead, a thirst for greater financial freedom, or just a "little" taste of the luxuries of life.

In the midst of these circumstances we want to find bibli-cal *and* practical solutions to the problem of how a job fits in with family and ministry. The issue cannot be avoided by going into "full-time" Christian work: then *ministry is the job,* and suddenly a new set of even more complex problems arises. For instance, what if you do not like some of the requirements of your ministry/job? If you cannot successfully blend your Christian life and your secular job, almost certainly you will not succeed in vocational Christian service.

After thirteen and a half years in my secular job I did change to vocational Christian service. The pressures remained as heavy. I still struggled to sustain a consistent devotional life. The conflicts and problems were still present. People expressed gratitude for all I did in my ministry as a layman; now I am expected to do it — and to do it better than before. After all, I have more time, so I should do more.

I am still the same person with the same motives, attitudes, and limitations. Yet the lessons I learned in coping with my secular job are the same ones that help me now. This book is a reflection of many of those experiences.

Many questions and issues confront Christians in secular jobs:

• What can I do when I do not like my work but cannot change because of educational or financial restrictions?

• How can I do well in my job without "selling my soul" to the company?

• Why do I have so many conflicts with my supervisors?

• I feel guilty working at a secular job when I know I could be on the mission field. I get convicted whenever I attend a missions conference. What should I do?

• My job is so demanding that it takes fifteen or twenty extra hours a week just to keep up. It is hurting my family, but how can I refuse to do what my boss asks of me?

• I am always running scared, because if I do not do my job well, there are ten people waiting to take it. How can I overcome this anxiety and trust God?

• We have three children in college, so both my husband and I are working. But it really bothers me, since I have been admonished that this is wrong. Is it?

• I have tried many times to give the proper priorities to my family and to some type of outreach ministry, but I fail every time. My priorities get fouled up, my schedule gets disrupted. How can I attain consistency?

• By the time I work forty-to-fifty hours on my job, go to three or four church meetings a week, and carry out my church responsibilities, I have no time left for the family. What should I do?

• The children are in their teens and are rebelling. My job is finally paying off, and to succeed I need to give it 100 percent. Should I give up my career just for the children?

• How do I decide to change jobs or location?

• Is it wrong to be ambitious?

• Is there anything wrong with being "just a housewife"?

• I have been to several family seminars and am deeply convicted about my relationship to my family. But still, I have to put bread on the table. How can I achieve a balance?

• Is there anything wrong with working hard to get nice things for the family?

• If I did everything I am told I "must" do to be a successful parent, employee, and Christian, I would need one hundred extra hours in the week! Can it really be done?

• I am "just" a factory worker. What good am I to the kingdom of God?

This book deals with these questions. It will not give black and white, dogmatic answers to each one, but will provide scriptural and practical principles from which you can personally seek God's will.

For clarity, we need to define the key words in this book:

Job or work: That task or skill that is the main source of your financial income — what you are expected to do to receive pay.

Family: Your wife or husband, children, and the activities arising from your responsibilities to them.

Ministry: Your spiritual outreach to those outside your

family. It may be through your church, in your neighborhood, or through other organized or unorganized Christian endeavors.

Some may say "my job is my ministry!" or "my family is my ministry!" That is true. But for the purposes of this discussion, we will simply use the term *ministry* to refer to outside endeavors.

The Christian View of Society

Before looking at the Christian view of work, we need to ask whether there is a Christian view of society. Is all society bad? Should prophecies of doom govern our thinking about the world? No society in history has been truly Christian. Not even Israel maintained a godly perspective over an extended period of time. But all of us live in society, with its problems, evils, and benefits.

Society becomes "Christian" only as individuals in it become Christians and multiply. Then they permeate it with Christian views of government, business, economics, politics, and ethics. But that will never happen if the Christian hibernates from his society. We need to be in the world, but not conformed to the world (Rom. 12:2).

The Bible teaches several things about human society.

Society is established by God. God established human society with certain objectives. In Genesis 1:26 man was "to rule . . . over all the earth." He is to "be fruitful and multiply, and fill the earth, and subdue it." God also established concepts of government, order, and justice. These were distinct from spiritual rules of worship. So God's objectives for human society were —

> — to glorify Himself in all creation (Ps. 19:1-6);
> — to establish authority and order (Deut. 16:18-20);
> — to meet man's physical needs (Gen. 1:29,30; Deut. 15:2-14);
> — to establish concepts of justice and man's relationships (Exod. 20:1-17).

Society is not inherently evil. Human society is not inherently wrong or evil. People do evil things, not society; but people constitute the society. By God's sovereignty we were each born into a segment of total society and cannot escape from it, nor should we want to. However, we want to influence our society to good and not allow society to influence us adversely.

It is true that the world system (cosmos) is condemned in the New Testament. But the world system is not the same as society. Society is a grouping of people around a common goal (e.g., survival, business, or protection). This society can be deeply influenced by Satan's way of thinking as expressed in the world system.

Society provides an environment. Human society provides an environment in which God confronts man. Human society is the mechanism by which man lives and functions as a human being. In this process each man is then confronted by God about his purpose in life and his personal relationship to God and Christ. The prime tools of confrontation are —

— the Scriptures (specific revelation);
— the creation (general revelation);
— individual Christians sharing their faith (personalized revelation).

Society perpetuates the race. Human society is self-perpetuating and self-preserving. Everyone takes part in the sustenance of everyone else. Imagine several families performing certain functions for each other, such as growing food, sewing clothes, and repairing homes. Food is needed, so some are farmers. People get sick, so some are doctors. Houses are needed, so some are carpenters. In a primitive sense, specialized labor is needed for items that meet physical needs. Industrialization, corporations, and competition have changed the face of simple trading, but the idea remains the same.

Every person makes a contribution to society. Every occupation fills a need, or at least a want. Ultimately we are all dependent on one another.

So what is the Christian view of society? Society was divinely ordained by God for the purpose of sustaining His human creation. Therefore we must be vital and active participants in every area of society to reach people for Christ and to influence it to be more Christian in character. We are an *anti-pollution* influence on the society.

You may say, "That's a little too academic. I'm stuck here,

so just tell me how to survive." Yes, but you must realize that where you are "stuck" is a part of God's plan for you. Even more, you are a key part of God's plan for reaching a pagan society. His plan is for you to be *salt* and *light* in the society.

> You are the salt of the earth; but if the salt has become tasteless, how will it be made salty again? It is good for nothing any more, except to be thrown out and trampled under foot by men. You are the light of the world. A city set on a hill cannot be hidden. Nor do men light a lamp, and put it under the peck-measure, but on the lampstand; and it gives light to all who are in the house. Let your light shine before men in such a way that they may see your good works, and glorify your Father who is in heaven (Matt. 5:13-16).

Have you ever salted your food and accidentally dumped too much in one place? You could hardly stand to taste it, could you? Salt must gently permeate the whole thing. Concentrated it tastes terrible; scattered out it gives flavor and savor to the food. So God wants Christians spread out in every neighborhood, institution, and occupation. Non-Christians should *taste* Christ by observing your life. What kind of flavor do you give as you work in your job?

Salt has another use. Gathered in large quantities it is a preservative. Unfortunately we often interpret salting society as Christians gathering together. The result? Preserved or pickled Christians! We must be out in the middle of society, where we find the real needs.

What about *light*? You are to be that too — in the middle of darkness. People need to *see* Christ in us by how we work, act, and react. When a candle is covered with a cup, it goes out. When you cover up as a Christian, you risk spiritual stagnation. Be out in the open, vulnerable to the scrutiny of every non-Christian.

Allow people to *taste* and *see* Christ in you. Be salt: permeate society with the taste of Christ. Be light: let society see Christ in you.

Can a Christian actually change even part of society? Here is a striking example.

Luming is a petite Filipino in her early thirties, very

feminine with a quiet, modest demeanor. A competent architect working for the government, until recently she was in the department that designed all the schools and government buildings in the province of Rizal. After design, it was the procedure that the projects be turned over to another department for bidding and construction.

Out of personal interest she followed the progress of one set of buildings designed to be built on a landfill area. She noticed that the contract was let for a much lower price than it would cost to build. Upon writing a memo to her boss, she was told, "Just mind your own business." But being a committed Christian and a citizen, it was her business.

Luming visited the site and found that the contractor had moved the building to a place not requiring a landfill — but it was not government property. This allowed the contractor to bid lower and still pocket a good deal of money. She marched up to the contractor and told him to cease and desist on the building. He told her it was out of her hands and none of her business. Obviously government officials were involved in a payoff.

Next Luming addressed a letter to the governor. It was bounced back before reaching him, with the warning that if she persisted in sending the memo through, her brother would lose his job. After discussing the situation with her brother, who was also a Christian, she sent the memo through. She was called in to explain the matter to the governor, and the contract was rescinded. Her brother did lose his job, and she was warned by others that if she persisted in this kind of honesty, she would never be promoted.

But Luming chose to live her life before God in the knowledge that she will ultimately answer to Him. Her department allowed no dishonest transactions. And this was through the influence of one woman who based her work on God's principles.

Ironically, Luming has since been promoted and is now division chief in charge of low-cost housing and subdivisions in the entire province. She also has a second responsibility as assistant to the governor's chief executive officer. Luming has changed her society by demonstrating a unique blend of professional competence and godly commitment.

The View of Work in the Old Testament

In the Old Testament work was highly honored, especially skilled labor. People who could make things — such as silversmiths, stonecutters, carpenters, cloth makers — were especially respected.

Throughout the Old Testament these principles stand out:

Everyone should work. There was honor in labor. Exodus 34:21 gives this command: "You shall work six days, but on the seventh day you shall rest; even during plowing time and harvest you shall rest." Emphasis is usually placed on resting one day a week. But note that it says, "You *shall* work six days." That is a command, not a choice. Idleness was condemned. Every man contributed his part in supporting his family. In Proverbs 6:6-8 God commands us to observe the ant and learn: the ant works hard to gather food to sustain life. Work is clearly an essential part of life.

Working hard is good. The Proverbs are filled with admonitions about hard work. "He also who is slack in his work is brother to him who destroys" (18:9). "Laziness casts into a deep sleep, and an idle man will suffer hunger" (19:15). The Old Testament condemns laziness and commends hard work.

Work is an integral part of life. This concept stemmed from the high view of responsibility to one's own family. Failing to provide for them made a man an outcast from the community. Every Jewish child was required to train for a manual occupation. In the beginning "the LORD God took the man and put him into the garden of Eden to cultivate it and keep it" (Gen. 2:15). William Barclay noted,

> To a Jew work was essential — work was of the essence of life. The Jews had a saying that "he who does not teach his son a trade teaches him to steal." A Jewish rabbi was the equivalent to a college lecturer or professor, but according to Jewish law he must take not a penny for teaching; he must have a trade at which he worked with his hands and by which he supported himself. So there were rabbis who were tailors and shoemakers and barbers and bakers and even performers. Work to a Jew was life.[1]

Work was satisfying. Man was not made to dread labor,

but to be fulfilled by the creation of his hands or mind. "The sleep of the working man is pleasant, whether he eats little or much" (Eccl. 5:12). "In all labor there is profit" (Prov. 14:23). "And I have seen that nothing is better than that man should be happy in his activities [work], for that is his lot" (Eccl. 3:22).

All legal professions were honorable. We see approval of all kinds of work:

laboring	(1 Kings 5:7-18)
manual skills	(Exod. 36:1,2)
business/managerial	(Daniel, Moses)
mental/scientific	(Daniel)

Some professions were "illegal" or dishonorable. These included prostitution, lending at high interest, any business which cheated or took advantage of the poor, or any business conducted dishonestly.

The View of Work in the New Testament

Work is assumed in the New Testament to be a normal mode of life for everyone. None of the Old Testament concepts are repealed, but all are emphasized, with additional stress on the person's attitude toward his job and employer. So even in the context of grace, there is no escaping the responsibility of work. In fact, now it is not just work, but how *well* one does his job.

Consider these additional key principles in the New Testament:

No work, no eat. Second Thessalonians 3:10 says, "If anyone will not work, neither let him eat." That is a tough statement. Where is our social compassion? In a day of unemployment compensations and socialized subsidies, Paul would not be very popular at the polls with that platform — even among Christians. But it says, "If anyone *will* not work. . . ." This signifies that there is an option. Paul is not dealing with the sick, elderly, or disabled, who have no choice. This rule applies to an individual who decides not to work — who is too lazy, too choosy, or too undependable to hold a job. Verse 14 goes on to say that we are not to associate with the man who refuses to work and becomes a sponge to society. There are valid reasons for being unemployed, and we are responsible to uphold each other in those circumstances.

Provide for your family. "But if any one does not provide for his own, and especially for those of his household, he has denied the faith, and is worse than an unbeliever" (1 Tim. 5:8). That is a big responsibility. A Christian must provide for the physical needs of his family. If he does not, his testimony is ruined. The emphasis here is on needs, not luxuries. In any society the only way to provide justly for the family is to work.

Be an obedient and submissive employee. In Colossians 3:22 Paul commands slaves to be obedient to their masters. In today's society this is the employee (though some probably feel like slaves in their jobs). Can you be submissive and obedient while participating in strikes and protests and demanding your "rights"? There is no simple answer to that question. The key is to do what is legal in your society and does not conflict with Scripture, and to come to a conviction about your participation in these activities. But be sure you have a clear conscience before God in your actions (Acts 24:16).

What are your rights? Did Jesus demand His rights? The one clear guideline in your job is to be faithful, obedient, and submissive. To the soldier John commanded, "Be content with your wages" (Luke 3:14). When you obey this command to be submissive, you will be mistreated at times. In similar circumstances Jesus set this example: "And while being reviled, He did not revile in return; while suffering, He uttered no threats, but kept entrusting Himself to Him who judges righteously" (1 Peter 2:23). On the other hand, in reaction to cheating and unlawful use of the temple, He overturned the moneychangers' tables and drove them out (Matt. 21:12,13). Each circumstance must be decided on its own merits.

Be a just and fair employer. "Masters, grant to your slaves justice and fairness, knowing that you too have a Master in heaven" (Col. 4:1). If you are an employer, you have an even greater responsibility to be just and fair to those who work for you. You are to pay them their wages fairly and promptly (Lev. 19:13). You are to look out for their concerns. You are to consider their rights and be responsive to their needs and requests.

Make excellence your work standard. Jesus worked as a carpenter — but He was not just a carpenter, He was God. Paul worked as a tentmaker — but he was not just a tentmaker, he was the Apostle to the Gentiles. Peter worked as a fisherman — but he was not just a fisherman, he was the Apostle to the Jews. Lydia worked as a cloth dyer — but she was not just a cloth dyer, she was a witness and a woman of hospitality. Do you think those persons followed these scriptural principles? Do you follow them?

Excellence in Work

- "I'd rather deal with the non-Christian in business. Too many Christians have really disappointed me in their dealings."

- "He may be a Christian, but he really doesn't do good work."

- "He claims to be a Christian, but I know atheists who work harder and do better work than he does."

Have you heard statements like that? Of course you have. Sadly enough, they are often true. You may argue that there are many non-Christians who do poor work. True. But we are a "chosen" people; there is a special mark and responsibility on us as Christians. You cannot be just an ordinary worker. "Whatever you do, do your work heartily, as for the Lord rather than for men" (Col. 3:23).

You represent Jesus Christ to the world, not just by your speech and morality, but also by your *work*. If you are *salt* and *light* to the world, you must be *salt* and *light* in your work too.

Between my junior and senior years in college I worked for Boeing Aircraft Co. as an engineering draftsman. As a Christian I felt the responsibility to witness to my co-workers, and witness I did — on the job, during work hours, when I and they were to be producing work for the company. What an impact I had! It was even noticed by the boss, who reprimanded me for not working! I learned a valuable lesson, but not till I had tarnished my "real" witness on the job. Moreover, no one came to Christ. In fact, I would hate to hear what they said behind my back.

> Do you see a man skilled in his work? He will stand before kings; he will not stand before obscure men (Prov. 22:29).
> I passed by the field of the sluggard, and by the vineyard of the man lacking sense; and behold, it was completely overgrown with thistles, its surface was covered with nettles, and its stone wall was broken down. When I saw, I reflected upon it; I looked, and received instruction (Prov. 24:30-32).

God expects excellence. He does not expect you to be a "superworker" or one who has no limitations; but He does expect you to do the best you possibly can.

What will be the results of your doing your work excellently? Here are a few:

- You will have a better witness.
- You will have more job security.
- You will be promoted or paid more.
- You will have greater job satisfaction.

As you see, there is much in it for you.

The Bible clearly teaches that work is right and good in life and society and that it must be done God's way. But knowledge alone cannot show you how to solve some of the knotty problems you are likely to encounter, so read on.

Discussion Questions

1. What is the biblical basis for secular work?
2. Is the "work ethic" Christian or cultural?
3. Is there a significant difference between work in the Old Testament and the New?
4. Discuss the purpose of society. How much effort should a Christian give to changing it?
5. What are some specific ways a Christian can change his or her society?
6. Discuss the concepts of Colossians 3:22 – 4:1. Does this apply to the Christian worker today?
7. What are the boundaries between loyalty to employer and loyalty to a union?
8. How can you help correct injustices in the labor world?
9. Discuss the meaning and context of 1 Thessalonians 4:11,12.
10. Under what conditions should the church support someone who is not working?

CHAPTER 2

THE CHRISTIAN VIEW
OF CIRCUMSTANCES

FROM TIME to time, everyone finds himself in difficult — indeed, miserable — circumstances. Some people struggle with adverse conditions far more frequently than others. The job is too demanding, the relationships on the job are difficult, trouble is brewing in the home, work hours are too long, money is tight, you have lost your job, you dislike the community in which you live, or your work has become boring and dissatisfying. When one or more of these things happen, we are plagued with the malady that I call . . .

The Grass-Is-Greener Syndrome

Do you believe the myth that changing your circumstances will solve your problems? This solution has been attempted many times and has failed, but still it persists even among those who have tried it. We mistakenly feel that the problem is outside ourselves and that changing our location, job, or surroundings will make things different. We make the change, but the problems return and we are no better off than before.

We are all familiar with the proverb that "the grass is greener on the other side of the fence." We feel if we could just be somewhere else, things would be better. But they seldom are. Changing your circumstances will not generally solve your problems. Most problems are of our own making or are generated within ourselves.

Could it be that God has placed you in some circumstances for your benefit and teaching? Could it be that He does not want you to escape, but to learn how to live in those circumstances? The immediate impulse in any difficulty is to run to avoid the situation. If we cannot run, we become bitter and complain about our plight. The bitterness deepens and we find ourselves in despair. In the whole process we lose our perspective of what God is doing in our lives. We question why God could let us experience these difficulties.

King Solomon spent his entire lifetime trying to find satisfying circumstances. He desperately searched for some situation that would make him happy. He never found it. His conclusion in the Book of Ecclesiastes was that "all is vanity." He tried to make circumstances fit his desires rather than allow God to be his total satisfaction in the existing situation.

Paul had the right response to circumstances. He said, "I have learned to be content in whatever circumstances I am. I know how to get along with humble means, and I also know how to live in prosperity; in any and every circumstance I have learned the secret of being filled and going hungry, both of having abundance and suffering need" (Phil. 4:11,12).

Paul had reconciled himself to . . .

Reality — Living Life as It Is

Escaping from circumstances usually means escaping from reality. We do not want to face life as it really is. We live in the future hoping that things will change, or in the past wishing that things were as they used to be. To live full and meaningful lives, we must live in the present.

If you are married and experiencing difficulties, you cannot go back to being single. If you have children and that responsibility weighs heavily on you, you still must meet the needs of your family. If you are having problems in your job now, you will likely encounter similar problems in another job. If you are having conflicts with people in your church, you will probably have conflicts in another church. Everywhere you turn, the pressure of reality confronts you.

But that is God's plan. God's objective is to use the pressures of real life to cause us to turn to Him. In John 16:33 Jesus promises constant pressure. "In the world you have tribulation, but take courage; I have overcome the world." The word *tribulation* is the same word used for pressing out the wine from the grapes. This verse could be translated "in the world you have pressure." We will never be able to escape those pressures, but we can have peace and fulfillment in the midst of them. Jesus says to "take courage," not to "run away"; because He has overcome the world, we can successfully endure that stress.

The beginning of John 16:33 teaches that we can have peace in spite of pressure. The peace comes in knowing that God is in charge and all our circumstances are divinely ordained by Him. Your reaction to circumstances reveals your spiritual maturity. Do you get angry? Do you become discouraged? Are you fearful? Although it is wrong to be angry with God for a set of circumstances, it is not wrong to ask why they exist. God has some purpose in every event He brings into your life.

Circumstances — God's Training Program for You

If anyone had a right to be bitter against God, it was Joseph (Gen. 37–47). He simply told the truth, and his brothers became furious and planned to kill him. Deciding that it would be wrong to take his life, they sold him as a slave into Egypt and deceived their elderly father into thinking he was dead. Joseph worked his way up in the household of Potiphar to a position of high responsibility. Moreover, he did this by excellent performance of his work and a right relationship with God. "And the LORD was with Joseph, so he became a successful man. And he was in the house of his master the Egyptian. Now his master saw that the LORD was with him and how the LORD caused all that he did to prosper in his hand" (Gen. 39:2,3).

Then Potiphar's wife tried to seduce him. When he refused, she made a false accusation, and Joseph was dismissed from his job and thrown into prison. There, even as a prisoner, he rose to a position of responsibility. God brought the Pharaoh's baker and butler into prison, and Joseph interpreted each of their dreams. Later the Pharaoh himself called for Joseph to interpret his dream and subsequently made Joseph the second ruler in the entire land of Egypt.

What if Joseph had become bitter and had sulked and complained against God? Would he ever have won the respect of those around him? I doubt it. In all these circumstances, he was treated unjustly, but God ultimately blessed him. Instead of getting an ulcer, he got honor. Instead of complaining, he complied. Instead of appealing through the courts, he became a faithful slave and servant. But Joseph could not have done this had he not understood that God had ordained the circumstances and was preparing him for the future. Are you willing to allow your circumstances to prepare you for the future?

Rather than giving you success and ease, God is first interested in changing your character to become more like Jesus Christ. Then He will use you to reach out to others.

What are some things that God might be trying to teach you through your circumstances? Here are a few possibilities:

1. If you are having conflicts with your boss, God may be trying to teach you something about *biblical submission to authority*.

2. If you are in very tight financial circumstances, God may be trying to teach you something about *generosity* or *materialism*.

3. If you are in conflict with your husband or wife, God may be teaching you something about the *biblical view of marriage*.

4. If you are being unjustly treated at your job, He may be teaching you how to *be at peace* in difficult circumstances.

5. If you are bored and discouraged in your job, He may be teaching you something about *patience* and *perseverance*.

6. If you are without a job, He may be teaching you *dependence on Him* and causing you to reevaluate your *priorities and objectives*.

7. If you are under pressure on your job because you have not done your work well, He may be teaching you something about *faithfulness* and *dependability*.

8. If you are experiencing fear and insecurity in your job, He may be teaching you *dependence on God* and finding your *security in Him.*

This list could go on, but in all these circumstances several key points begin to stand out.

• God is sovereign in your circumstances.

• Be patient in waiting for God to resolve the circumstance. Let Him get your attention so you can learn the lesson He intends to teach you.

• God wants to change your character, personality, and attitude toward Him and toward others.

• God wants you to find your total peace and contentment in your relationship with Him, through His Word and prayer.

Many know the words of Romans 8:28: "And we know that God causes all things to work together for good to those who love God, to those who are called according to His purpose." But do you know the experience of that verse? God has a specific purpose in every circumstance. The prerequisites are that you love God and are in His will right now. Romans 8:28 is not just a cop-out on reality or a glib reply to be given to others in distress. This verse causes us to understand that God is trying to get our attention and that He will ultimately turn adverse circumstances to good. He does not guarantee a total understanding of what He is doing and why, but He guarantees that He is acting on our behalf.

Are you in a particularly bad circumstance? What can you do to discover what God is trying to teach you? Take a piece of paper and briefly answer the following questions as a start:

1. What is the circumstance? Be brief, but describe it specifically.

2. How did the circumstance develop?

3. From your experience in the circumstance so far, what are some possible things God could be trying to teach you?

Now set that paper aside as we look at some other aspects of circumstances.

Attitude Toward Authority

A common cause of adverse circumstances is conflict with authority. Employee with employer. Worker with foreman. Wife with husband. Children with parents. Christian with spiritual leader. Conflict comes from pride: "Only by pride cometh contention" (Prov. 13:10 KJV). There is something deep within us that resents *any* kind of authority. We want to be independent. We don't want anyone to tell us what to do or how to do it.

Listen in on a conversation in the Lacey home. Randy is thirty-eight and an experienced machinist.

"Can you imagine the nerve of that punk kid?"

"Another run-in with that young engineer?" responded his wife.

"'Young engineer' is hardly the word! Ignorant would be better. I've got fifteen years' experience on those machines, and he thinks one course in college and a degree gives him the right to tell me how to do my job?"

"But, Randy, he is in charge of the shop and — "

"I don't care if he owns the place! I refuse to let him tell me how to do my job."

There was a long silence as he hung up his coat. His stomach hurt. He had a headache. Worse yet, he knew his attitude was wrong for a Christian. Then Jan quietly interrupted his thoughts.

"Randy, I wonder if there isn't a pattern to this. Two months ago you were upset because the pastor asked you to change the ushering methods. Three weeks ago you refused to work any overtime. Then you were upset for a week after you got that speeding ticket. It seems as if anytime someone tells you what to do, you get mad."

That really hurt. But as Randy reflected on it, he knew his wife was right: he resented instruction or authority of any kind.

Every person is under some kind of authority. We are all under the authority of government and laws. We are under the authority of our employer. We are under the authority of our church. In this context, however, I want to discuss primarily our response and attitude toward authority in the job. A common evidence of rebellion toward authority is griping and complaining — about the boss, the company, regulations, rules, and myriad other things that arise in the daily routine of work. The complaints may be valid, and you may be encountering unjust treatment. But the attitude of the Christian must be to "do all things without grumbling or disputing; that you may prove yourselves to be blameless and innocent, children of God above reproach in the midst of a crooked and perverse generation, among whom you appear as lights in the world" (Phil. 2:14,15).

"Are you telling me that a Christian is to be totally passive in his job and relationships to authority?" you ask. By no means. A Christian can discuss the facts of his job and bring grievances to the attention of management. But he is to do so in an orderly fashion within the system of that company. Bad circumstances normally do not develop from serious grievances, but rather from petty personal irritants. We complain to other employees, to our family and friends. Eventually the complaints affect our performance on the job, and we enter into a conflict with authority. Finally this conflict brings about circumstances that infect every aspect of our lives.

What is your attitude toward authority? Do you resent your foreman, your employer, or your company? How does that affect your attitude each day? Have you seen this resentment create circumstances that bring additional pressure upon you? God has ordained your relationship to that authority. When you rebel, you are really rebelling against God. This is true whether it is employer or government. If you have difficulty living in one authority structure, you will have difficulty in another. Some people have a history of problems with their supervisors. That is a sure sign of rebellion against God's established authority. Until your attitude is resolved to one which is biblical, you will never have real peace in your job.

> To love those below you is not so difficult. . . . You can love those below you without affecting your pride. Your posture is superior condescension, magnanimous moral conceit. But to love the man above you is different. To love him without flattery or self abasement, to love him without bitterness or resentment, to love him in the midst

of conflict and pain: to love the man above you is love's
highest hurdle — you cannot get over it alone. You cannot
do it without the Cross inside lifting you up.[1]

How "Bad" Circumstances Develop

An acquaintance of mine left his job under tense circumstances, and I could not understand why. In my casual contacts
with him, we seemed to get along just fine. Then I had an
opportunity to be in some business discussions with him.
Almost everything he said had a "barb" in it. Comments or
proposals were like a challenge to fight; he simply could not
speak in a normal tone that allowed for reasonable discussion.
It seemed that he was emotionally involved in every comment.

Some people have a way with words — no matter what
they say, they offend. Likewise, some have a knack for getting
themselves into difficult circumstances. Often there is a major
difficulty in their personal life, relationships, or home. Every
time the situation is discussed, the facts seem to be overwhelm-
ingly on their side as they see it. They are never at fault and
always seem to be getting a "bum deal." But though they don't
realize it, the circumstances were created by them.

Remember my statements about tribulation and pressure? Note that tribulation is not always persecution. I have
frequently encountered Christians who perennially seem to be
in the midst of conflict on their job or with their neighbors or in
their church — and they claim to be persecuted. Genuine
persecution in our society is unusual: we all undergo some
pressure as a result of our faith, but rarely is it persecution. In
some instances it may appear that an individual is being persecuted for his faith; but when the facts are known, they reveal he
has wrongly related his faith to his co-workers or friends. If you
display a belligerent or legalistic manner, for example, you will
undoubtedly evoke a hostile response.

In Galatians 6:7 we read that "whatever a man sows, this
he will also reap." Though our adverse circumstances are often
self-created, this does not change the fact that they exist. But
this can teach us a lesson in how to avoid similar circumstances
later. Sometimes we are in adverse circumstances because we
have sinned: we must live with the consequences of what we
have done. Let's be honest with God and with ourselves: when
our circumstances are a direct result of our sin, poor judgment,

attitudes, or personality, we must admit it. Then we must take steps to correct the cause and know what God wants to teach us from the circumstance.

Victory, Not Escape

Often our first response to tough circumstances is to plan a way of escape. We want to avoid bearing the responsibility for our actions. We want relief, not victory.

That philosophy is fine when we deal with sin: we do want to escape. But we also want the victory of keeping out of similar circumstances in the future.

Let us examine the passage in Philippians 4. Paul said, "I have learned to be content. . . ." This is not an automatic response. Contentment is not characteristic of human nature; it is not even natural to a Christian. It is a learned response. You strive for it. You appeal to God in prayer asking for it. You must learn to live at peace in your circumstances, especially those from which it is impossible to escape.

What does it mean to be content? Certainly it is not some zombielike state of indifference to the world about you. Nor is it wandering through life with a glassy-eyed look and a slightly pious smile — oblivious to the chaos around you. In fact, there may be great pain and difficulty in your circumstances. Contentment means you are persuaded that God is using those circumstances to teach and develop you. Also, that the circumstances were ordained by Him or at least permitted by Him if they result from your sin.

The specific context of Philippians 4:11 concerns money and standard of living. And that relates very closely to work. Our employment provides our finances. Paul said he could get along *with* money or *without* it. He stated that "in any and every circumstance" he had learned the secret of contentment. Paul followed this with one of the more familiar "crutch" verses in the New Testament — Philippians 4:13. "I can do all things through Him who strengthens me." Note that this "strengthening" and this "doing all things" come in the context of living in the circumstances God provides. You cannot glibly claim verse 13 without coming to grips with being satisfied where God has put you.

How do people try to escape? By leaving the scene? Not

always. I knew a student who escaped by sleeping all day and reading all night; he stopped going to all classes and flunked out. Some people try drugs or alcohol. Others immerse themselves in a hobby. Some even try to escape by becoming superactivists in the church. Still others try anything that helps them forget their real problems.

Suppose that you do choose to run and escape. Can it really be done? I believe not. God will pursue you, and you will soon find yourself in another set of circumstances in which He is trying to get your attention and teach you the same thing. Since you cannot escape, why don't you learn to have victory in your present circumstances? In Philippians 4:13 you are promised the strength for that victory. Take advantage of your situation and learn what God has for you in it.

When to Change Circumstances

Let us not think that there is never a time for voluntarily changing circumstances. In the normal course of finding God's will, there are many times when we definitely *should* change our circumstances. Indeed, circumstances can be an indication of God's directing us toward some other avenue of work, ministry, or location. In chapter 5 I focus on the matter of changing job, location, or career. Here I simply want to develop a process of evaluation of the circumstances we are in. The conclusion of that evaluation may be that we should move to change the circumstances. God frequently used circumstances to lead His people in new directions. Joseph came into Egypt as a result of adverse circumstances. Paul had a witness in Rome because of hostile conditions; he left certain locations of ministry when a situation became impossible. We must be sensitive to understand God's will and to know when a situation is hopeless.

By using the following practical guidelines, you can think through and evaluate your situation and what you should do:

1. Write out a few details of your circumstances. Be specific and simple.

2. Describe how the circumstances developed. Jot down a few key items that you can recall in the developing crises. From this you may be able to see where a critical incident occurred that turned good circumstances to bad.

3. What actions on your part may have precipitated some of the circumstances? Can you recall any incident that really aggravated the situation?

4. Was there sin on your part? Were the circumstances self-generated? Be brutally honest with yourself in this. If there was sin, simply bring it to God and confess it. It may be that you will also have to confess this to someone else to correct the problem.

5. What effect have these circumstances had on —
— your family;
— your spiritual life;
— your relationships with people?

If any of these concerns has been drastically affected, you cannot tolerate the status quo for long. Remember that the circumstances may not have caused these to be affected, but simply your *attitude* toward the circumstances.

6. What may God be trying to teach you through these circumstances? What has God taught you so far?

7. Are you willing to stay in the circumstances? This is critical, because God wants you to be in neutral to find His will. Therefore you need to be willing either to change the circumstances or to live in them.

8. What actions can you take to resolve circumstances? There may be specific things you can do right now. You may need to quit your job, apologize to someone, change jobs within your company, change your attitude toward authority, or do what the boss says instead of resisting his direction.

9. If you change the circumstance, would you be avoiding a lesson from God?

10. Write down two or three possible solutions to your adverse circumstances and then —
— pray over them;
— seek counsel from someone who is godly and whom you trust;
— make a decision on what you should do.

11. Take action now! The action may simply be to wait and endure your circumstances patiently. Whatever it is, do it with a clear conscience, knowing that God has directed and will bless you.

These steps of evaluation are by no means a "magic potion" that you can apply to find an easy solution. They merely will help you to be honest with yourself and with God. They will give you a basis on which to discern His will.

Discussion Questions

1. Why do people tend to run away from adverse circumstances?
2. Discuss ways a person can create adverse circumstances for himself.
3. What is legitimate authority? How much authority does an employer have?
4. What are evidences of rebellion toward authority?
5. When should a Christian change circumstances?
6. Why does God allow adverse circumstances? What should be our reaction to them?

CHAPTER 3

WHAT'S THE POINT?

DURING THE nation's economic recession of the mid-seventies, the construction business in Colorado Springs was especially hard hit. Many were losing their jobs, and business was slow. Friends of ours in the construction business were caught in the financial pinch. One evening they lingered to talk after a group gathering in our home. Instead of being depressed and despondent, they were happy, outgoing, and expressive of what God was doing in their lives. Their reactions were puzzling to us in view of their circumstances.

They told us, "Just today we sold our snowmobiles, some motorbikes, and other recreational equipment that we thought we just had to have when we had lots of money. Since we decided to sell these things, we have found that we didn't need them at all. In fact, our family is happier. This has really drawn us together much more than we ever expected. When we had ample money, it seemed as if we could buy anything we wanted for ourselves and for the kids. It just seemed like the right thing to do. But it didn't make us any happier. We have learned a real lesson."

The couple added that having the extra finances was actually a hindrance to them. It caused them to be more materialistic and more inclined to spend money unnecessarily.

The Lure of Materialism

Our entire society is plagued by the myth of materialism. TV, radio, and newspapers consistently promote the idea that getting *things* will make a person happy. Even after buying something we have worked hard to get and finding that it does not bring happiness, we still believe that the next little toy will do so. Men want a newer car, a better workshop, fancier tools, a new shotgun, or more stereo equipment. Women want a more modern kitchen, the latest furniture, a bigger house, or a new wardrobe. Children are no longer satisfied with homemade or self-created entertainment and toys, but must have the latest gimmick being advertised on TV or displayed in the stores.

An unfortunate development of this age is that all these things can be acquired immediately without money. The only requirement is a license for indebtedness in the form of a plastic credit card. The sad part of the whole cycle is that people are never satisfied. What will satisfy? Just a little bit more.

Possessing nice things, however, does not mean a person is materialistic. Having money does not mean a person is greedy. Buying a new car or a new home or a new wardrobe does not mean a person is misusing his money. The key lies in a person's attitude toward things. What is important to you? What is your objective in life? Is it to make yourself comfortable through material things? You can have virtually nothing in the way of possessions and yet be materialistic, greedy, and envious. Another person can have a mansion and every possible luxury available and still not be materialistic. It is a matter of heart attitude. In Matthew 6:33 we read, "But seek first His kingdom and His righteousness; and all these things shall be added to you."

Many of us find ourselves grasping for happiness and

fulfillment in a vicious circle of acquiring material things. When we finally run head-on into a wall of frustration and ask, "What's the point?" we begin seeking the true objectives of our lives.

God's Objectives for Every Christian

God did not create the world or man without purpose. Nor does He want life to be lived without direction. He wants us to have objectives for our lives — to know what we are doing and why. The question must be, "Is my objective the right one for me?" To judge rightness and wrongness we need a standard. God does have a discernible objective, clearly taught in the Scriptures. Our objectives must fit God's objectives for us and for the world.

First, God wants every Christian to be growing into the likeness and image of His Son, Jesus Christ. "For whom He foreknew, He also predestined to be conformed to the image of His Son" (Rom. 8:29). He wants us to be conformed in every aspect of our lives — thought, action, character, and attitude. This is, of course, a lifelong process.

Second, each Christian is a part of God's instrument for reaching out to the world with the gospel. "Go therefore and make disciples of all the nations, baptizing them in the name of the Father and the Son and the Holy Spirit, teaching them to observe all that I commanded you; and lo, I am with you always, even to the end of the age" (Matt. 28:19,20). We have a direct command from Jesus Christ to share the gospel as widely as possible.

Could anyone ask for two greater objectives? To reach the world for Christ and to become conformed to the likeness of Christ are goals that challenge every person to his greatest potential.

You may think that those objectives sound worthy but very impractical for someone in your circumstances. You would be right if God had not clearly decided how this is to be done. Every Christian in the world *can* have a significant part in sharing the gospel. And every Christian can be growing daily into the image of Christ. This leads us to two of the most crucial passages of this book. We want to see God's concept of witness and God's concept of discipleship.

Concepts of Witness

"If that's what a Christian is like, I don't want any part of it," said a man of a fellow worker. You do not need to decide *if* you will witness: you *are* a witness. The only question is whether your witness is for or against Christ.

Recall from chapter 1 that we are to be *salt* and *light* in our society. But we cannot be that kind of influence unless we are involved in every segment of society. The only places this can happen are in —
> — our job;
> — our neighborhood.

Have you ever wondered why you are a construction worker and not a doctor? Or a factory worker and not a factory manager? Or a teacher and not a bus driver? God has sovereignly placed you where you are with your particular ability, background, and circumstances. Because of the level of income in your job, you naturally buy or rent in certain neighborhoods. Whether we like it or not, neighborhoods segregate according to social and financial levels. Instead of envying those who have more than you have, thank God for placing you in both your job and your neighborhood so you can be salt and light for Christ where you are.

Of these two, the job is the more important in your witness. The only place close association is actually forced is on the job, so maximize your witness there. Because society is becoming more and more private, neighbors don't know each other as they once did. People isolate themselves in their backyards behind high fences. Many purposely avoid knowing others on their street. And the problem is compounded in that the average American moves every four or five years.

But don't give up in your neighborhood. Be a part of any activity there. Attend the PTA. Help in community social efforts. Invite your neighbors into your home. Help them when there is an illness or apparent need. When your children play with neighbors, use that as an opportunity to meet the parents. It can be done — if *you* make the effort. Women are often the most effective in making neighborhood contacts.

How do you actually witness on the job or in the neighborhood?

The most obvious way is by your *actions*. People see how you work and react to difficult situations. They see if you cheat your employer on the "little" things, if you get angry, or if you always protect your own interests. The way you work and act provides the opportunities to share verbally what you believe.

The second kind of witness is your *character* — the real person deep down inside. People do judge the kind of person you are. They tend to judge your motives to the extent that they perceive them.

"Jack doesn't say much, but he's got a heart of gold. He'd give you the shirt off his back."

"Bill talks a good line, but there's something phoney about him — he's trying to get the boss's job."

"Have you noticed that he works when the boss is around, but how lazy he is the rest of the time?"

Others are attracted or repelled by the kind of person they believe you are.

Two brothers became Christians in a small community. They were both involved in well-known firms. Both became very verbal about their new relationship in Christ, yet people believed the one and ridiculed the other. Why? Because in one brother they saw a distinct change in character and business methods. In the other they only heard talk. God must change us on the inside or our witness will be ignored.

The third witness is what you *say*. Through words you communicate your faith in Christ. Do you know how to share your faith? Can you share your personal testimony? Can you turn a conversation from ordinary matters to spiritual things? Are you timid or unsure about telling others of Christ? I strongly recommend two practical books that clearly teach effective methods of witnessing: *Winning Ways* by LeRoy Eims, and *How to Give Away Your Faith* by Paul Little.[1]

However, the whole purpose of relating well to your work is not only for your personal happiness, but also for your effective witness. Therefore several factors will help you in your witness on the job and in your neighborhood, as follows:

1. If you are going to be a witness, you must first know where you stand with God. Have you personally received Jesus Christ as your Savior? If not, I urge you to do that now. All the

principles of this book are based on the premise that you know Christ and are a Christian. You need that assurance of salvation to communicate your own beliefs with conviction.

2. Write out your personal testimony. Doing so helps you to be concise and able to select carefully the facts of your spiritual background and the gospel in brief time. You should be able to give your testimony in two to four minutes. Don't preach, just share the facts.

3. Learn to share the gospel clearly using two or three methods. You may use tracts, but I recommend that you learn to use an aid such as the Bridge illustration of The Navigators or the Four Spiritual Laws of Campus Crusade for Christ. Learn to sketch these verbally without referring to a printed publication. Practice this with a Christian friend before sharing it with a non-Christian.

4. Never witness during your working time. Use coffee breaks and lunchtimes to talk about Christianity. Adhere to this guideline: Does my witnessing to a co-worker prevent either of us from accomplishing a task for the company? For instance, you certainly could talk as you are driving a truck or car from one work site to another.

5. Develop friendships with those on the job. Be a good listener. Be genuinely interested in their affairs. In that process do not hesitate to let your stand as a Christian be known. But also, do not force others to listen to your witness. Once they know your stand, they can ask questions — and they will, if your life is attractive.

6. Look for opportunities to share the gospel. Be alert to times of turmoil or difficulty in another person's life when he would most likely be open to considering Jesus Christ. Having opportunities means nothing unless you actually take advantage of them. Be bold. Don't get so involved in developing a friendship that you don't share the gospel. In some circumstances you might share the gospel after the first or second conversation with someone. Then continue to cultivate the friendship.

7. Invite co-workers to your home for dinner and conversation. Be active with them socially.

8. Serve other people. Be alert to opportunities to be a physical help. Lift their load at work. Help them with a project

at home. Take care of their children in a time of need.

As I was writing these words, I saw my neighbor in his backyard, moving a scaffolding for painting. My immediate thought was that I should offer to help him, but my preference was to keep on writing and not be interrupted. I sat and struggled about what I should do. Ironically, I was writing a section on how to witness to neighbors and fellow workers. I did finally go out and offer to help, and he was grateful.

9. Use your home for investigative Bible studies. Make them short-term, perhaps one hour a week for four weeks. Numerous materials are available, and I recommend The Navigators' *How to Lead an Evangelistic Bible Study*.

10. Be involved in whatever social functions you can. Many Christians separate themselves so strongly from the world that they never become involved with co-workers apart from the job. You can attend events like company picnics: you need not compromise your standards of conduct, but your presence is important.

What about witnessing through the church's evangelism program and organized door-to-door evangelism? It is certainly good to be involved in that broad outreach in the neighborhoods. But it *must not* replace personal witnessing where you work and where you live. Anyone can go door-to-door, but only you can witness where God has placed you.

Concepts of Discipleship

Everyone expects a baby to act like a baby. But when a five-year-old still acts like a baby and has not grown physically and mentally, there is great concern. It becomes obvious to everyone that something is dreadfully wrong. When a person is a brand new Christian, no one expects him to evidence Christian maturity, but unfortunately many people remain Christian babies for years.

God intended that we should grow spiritually. He wants us to become mature, committed, and productive members of the body of Christ. "We are to *grow* up in all aspects into Him, who is the head, even Christ" (Eph. 4:15). "Like newborn babes, long for the pure milk of the word, that by it you may grow in respect to salvation" (1 Peter 2:2). God wants growth, not stagnation. Growth like this is often called discipleship: we are to be committed disciples of Jesus Christ. The word *disciple* in the Greek simply means "learner." To grow involves both learning and doing. Knowledge alone is not sufficient. We must apply what we learn to our daily living. We must be obedient Christians, not just knowledgeable Christians.

Many factors are involved in discipleship. Walter A. Henrichsen provides an excellent guide to being a disciple in his book *Disciples Are Made — Not Born*.[2] Here is a checklist on some of the basic aspects of discipleship:

• A disciple has a regular daily time of reading God's Word and prayer. This is a devotional time, not a study time (1 Peter 4:7).

• A disciple is actively involved with other Christians in fellowship. This can include involvement in a church and in small groups (Heb. 10:25).

• A disciple studies the Word of God regularly. He is increasing in his knowledge of what the Bible says (2 Tim. 2:15).

• A disciple applies the Word to his life. He is making "lordship" decisions — allowing God to control every aspect of his life. He is actively turning away from sin (Luke 9:23; Prov. 4:14,15).

• He is sharing his faith with non-Christians (1 Peter 3:15).

• The disciple's place in the home and family is based on Scripture — he is fulfilling the scriptural role, whether as husband or wife. He is training his children in a godly manner (Eph. 5:22–6:4).

• The disciple is developing in his job and work and is relating to it biblically (Eph. 6:5-9).

This list does not require that you be perfect in each of these ways. It means you are a learner — one who is growing. In a simplified sense, we could say a disciple is one who is in daily fellowship with Christ in His Word and is attempting to put it into practice in his life.

If you start trying to apply some of the principles in this book in your job and neglect the basics of your personal walk with God, you will fail. As you grow in discipleship, you will be continually confronted with lordship decisions (putting God first) that will not be easy. Many of those lordship decisions will be related to your work. For example, you may be asked to do something unethical or dishonest; our response is a lordship decision. Or, there may be much opportunity for overtime and extra pay; but if you need to spend more time with your family or in Christian ministry, it is a lordship decision to forego the extra money. If those first points of discipleship are actively experienced in your life, you will have the foundation you need to respond properly in the lordship decision.

Is Christ Lord of your life now? Are there aspects that you are knowingly withholding from Him? If there are, I urge you to settle them with God now. Have you committed your job to God? You may have to do that before much of this book makes sense to you. In many ways discipleship precedes witness. Without discipleship our witness becomes hypocritical. And no one likes a hypocrite — especially non-Christians.

I question whether anyone can be a true disciple without having a biblical relationship to his job. The disciple knows that God has put him where he is and wants him to enjoy what he is doing. God has put him there for the purpose of reaching out to the lost. Are you a disciple in your job?

Setting Objectives That Work

Every decision we make is based upon one of the following:

• **Habit.** With habits, no premeditation is involved. We do a certain thing because we have done it before. The habit can be either bad or good, can serve us or work against us.

• **Urgency and fear.** We do some things because of the consequences of not doing them. We pay certain bills promptly and put off others. We get to work on time, but not to church on time.

• **Desire.** Some things we do because we simply enjoy doing them. The basis may be lust; it may have nothing to do with importance or need. This can be an overwhelming motivation and at times even irrational.

• **Expediency.** We may do something, not because we

want to or because it is the best action, but simply because we want to achieve a certain goal. People cheat because it is the easiest way to attain the objective. Lies are often a result of expediency. This motivation is the outworking of the philosophy that the end justifies the means.

● **Chosen direction.** We choose some actions, either on our own, by God's direction, or by the direction of someone else. These decisions are based upon correct objectives and priorities. We know why we do them, and we have made a conscious choice about them.

The first four of these motivations do not require deliberation — they just happen. Only the fifth is a deliberate option. At times each of these has a proper place: we need not ponder the merits of brushing our teeth; we do not need to make a decision whether to eat at mealtime; we feel free to do some things from desire, as for recreation; taking short-cuts may be wise when sin and moral or legal conflicts are not involved. But we want to operate our lives on a more substantial basis than the first four motivations alone provide. We want to base our lives on objectives that relate to God's goals for us. We want to govern our lives by personal decision and choice.

Let's define an objective: *It is a specific goal to be reached at the end of a considered period of time.*

Here are examples:

● To read the Bible through in one year;

● To finish a job-related correspondence course by September 1;

● To take my son on two camping trips this year.

Are these objectives? Only in a limited sense. They are more accurately viewed as activities that we might do to reach some objectives. Let's try again:

● To grow in my knowledge of the Scriptures by—

— reading the Bible through in one year;

— studying the Gospel of John and Galatians this year.

● To increase my proficiency on the job in regard to supervising within the next nine months by —

— completing a supervisors correspondence course by July 31;

— praying daily for the men I supervise.

- To deepen my relationship with my son this year by —
  — taking him on two camping trips;
  — going to at least four of his team's basketball games.

Do you see the difference? The camping trip is not crucial. My relationship with my son is the important thing.

There are two kinds of objectives:

- Short range (weeks or months to two years);

- Long range (two years and beyond).

There are four categories of objectives:

- Personal/spiritual (your relationship to God);

- Family;

- Job;

- Ministry (outwardly directed spiritual activities such as church, Bible studies, witnessing).

Why do we need objectives at all? Because most of us live in a frenzy of "good" activities without even asking, "Why am I doing this?"

John was a typical activist in our church. He was involved in everything — taught Sunday school, served on the board, attended every meeting, held evangelistic Bible studies in his home, and participated in special projects. Finally his body ran down. He lost sleep and became ineffective at work, and his family was rebelling.

"What's your main objective in life, John?"

"Well, that's a hard question. I guess to become a man of God, to be a good father, and to do my part in sharing Christ with the unsaved."

"Those are really good objectives. Let's take the first one. Are you doing personal Bible study?"

"Uh, not really. I just use the teaching manual for Sunday school and follow a prepared course in the evangelistic study."

"How's your prayer time?"

"Ouch! Pretty slim."

"Are you doing anything that would help you become a man of God?"

"Let's see . . . "

"John, it's obvious that your objective is *not* to be a man of God. That's a pipe dream!"

John had no objectives. Note that he did not even mention his job. It is all too easy to be "doing" with no purpose except to fulfill other people's expectations.

Another important factor is priorities. Priorities determine what we do first, second, or not at all when we have a choice. They are based on our objectives. We cannot have priorities without implying some objectives. But we will discuss priorities later. Let's get specific and practical on objectives now.

With a blank piece of paper before you, take a moment to ask God to help you set some realistic objectives.

1. Quickly jot down several things you would like to see happen in your life, family, and job in the next ten years. Don't linger on this — just write some thoughts (e.g., be a good husband, change careers, have a significant prayer life). As you write short-term objectives, you can see if they fit any of these ten-year goals. Establish and complete short-term goals for several months before trying to settle on specific long-term ones.

2. Let us brainstorm on some short-range objectives. Think in terms of one-to-three months. Divide your page under headings of the four categories (personal/spiritual, family, job, and ministry). Start jotting down random ideas on possible objectives for your life; these may reflect your known needs, wants, or hopes. Place them in the proper categories. Don't ponder too much, but write down your wildest (or most insignificant) thoughts. Take only ten or fifteen minutes for this list; you can revise it later. Try to put at least five or six things in each category.

3. Beside each item put a code to show if it is an objective (OB) or activity (A). (See figure 1.)

4. Select carefully one objective (and only one) that you consider the most important in each category. List these four items on a separate sheet of paper.

5. This is the crucial stage. For each of the four objectives, write down *one* activity you can do in the next month to help achieve that goal. Make each activity simple, realistic, and workable. For instance, if your goal is to develop your prayer

Personal/Spiritual	Family
OB Develop a consistent devotional life.	A Pray with my wife
A Pray 10 minutes daily	OB Develop a deeper relationship with my son.
A _____	OB _____
OB _____	A _____
	A _____

Job	Ministry
A Get to work on time	OB Witness to my neighbors
OB Have a better testimony at work	A Ask our next door neighbor for dinner
OB Do better work	OB Improve teaching in Sunday School
A _____	A _____
OB _____	A _____

Figure 1

life, do not prescribe an activity of praying one hour a day for thirty days: you would certainly fail. Rather, set a goal of praying five minutes a day, at least five days each week. If your objective is to do better work on your job, don't list an activity of increasing your production 100 percent; rather, seek to correct one aspect in which you know you have been lax in the production system.

6. Now choose from among the four categories the one best for you to begin tomorrow. After one week, take another category and work on the two together for another week. In the third week, add the third activity. Do the three for a week, and add the fourth. In other words, do not attempt to achieve all your objectives at once, but gradually increase your efforts.

7. When each activity has been in effect for a month, evaluate your progress. Now you can make adjustments. Your activities should develop into good habits and attitudes so they no longer take great conscious effort.

8. As you succeed in setting short-term objectives and activities, you can become more ambitious and go for longer times or more significant objectives. Return to your original list and determine the next most important objective in each category. You may also want to add some new ideas to this list now.

The key: Keep it simple. Do not try to do everything at once. Be realistic and discipline yourself to do what you set out to accomplish. "Desire realized is sweet to the soul" (Prov. 13:19).

A warning: Don't expect miracles. This is just a tool to help you put meaning and direction into your life. Nothing can replace that daily communication with God in which you find His will for you for the day. But if you have prayed over your objectives, the two will likely coincide.

9. This is more difficult. Over a period of three months, *eliminate* one activity that does not fit any of your objectives. You cannot keep adding activities to an already full schedule without eliminating something.

10. Say no to at least one activity in which you are asked to participate that does not contribute to your objective. Get into

the habit of being selective. Never be afraid to say no.

Now you have a start. Work at it until you feel comfortable with setting objectives (but not too comfortable, for a little pressure is helpful).

A final suggestion to keep you "honest": *Have someone check up on you!*

Time and Priorities

"Which is most valuable — time or money?" asked the young student.

"Ask any rich old man," replied the millionaire.

Time presses us. It frustrates us. It disappears. There never seems to be enough. Even when we use it well, we wonder if it could have been used better. Time spent with no objective is discouraging. If we have no clear objectives, life is absurd.

> We go, and keep on going,
> Until the object of the game
> Seems to be
> To go and keep on going.
>
> We do, and keep on doing,
> Until we do
> Without knowing — without feeling.
>
> Is there no time to stop and reflect?
> Is there no time to stop?
> Is there no time?
>
> If we stopped, would we keep on going?
> If we reflected, would we keep doing
> What we do?
>
> For what we have done
> And where we have gone
> Is dissolved into oblivion
> Or strung on the meaningless chain
> Of half remembered this and that
> If there is no reflection.
>
> In all our doing have we done anything?
> In all our going have we been anywhere?
>
> — *Author unknown*

Priorities without objectives are meaningless. Objectives without priorities are future. Both require time for fulfillment.

Let us be practical. Most of our time is already taken by our job or other mandatory responsibilities. We have only a limited amount over which we have control — our *discretionary* time. How much is there? On working days:

8 hours	work
½ hour	lunch
1 hour	transportation
1 hour	two other meals (breakfast, dinner)
8 hours	sleep
1 hour	miscellaneous mandatory items

19½ hours

This leaves about 4½ hours per working day for us to use as we desire — or 22½ hours each work week. Now assume there are 8 hours of discretionary time on Saturday and 6 on Sunday (excluding church), for a total of 36½ hours per week. Add a few household projects, shopping, taking the children to various activities, and some other "necessities," and we are down to about 24 hours. Not much left of the original 168 hours, is there? These 24 hours are available to fulfill our objectives other than job goals. But notice: that is equivalent to three full working days, or 60 percent of the time we put into our jobs!

All we have to do to blow it all is to throw in a few meaningless activities — an hour a day of TV, or one meeting that does not meet our objectives — and we have just destroyed half of our discretionary time. We must have priorities, or we will just muddle through life "hoping it will all work out."

As a young Air Force lieutenant, I was involved in many activities on the base. I taught a high school class, ran the youth program, was chairman of the junior officers' council, sang in a choral society, played sports, led a Bible study, maintained a hi-fi and electronics hobby and held a demanding round-the-clock job. I rarely saw my son. I left my wife with the entire home responsibility. I was not wandering; I was running at top speed — in every direction at once, with no objectives and no explicit priorities. My wife tried to slow me down, but I would not listen. I had to run into a wall to learn the lesson: Listen to your wife. Wives often are more perceptive than we husbands in seeing the outcome of our activity cycle, especially as it relates to the children.

I finally ended up flat on my back from physical exhaustion. God got my attention, and I vowed to set my objectives and live on priorities. It was a turning point in my life.

A very basic list of priorities includes —

— your personal walk with God;
— your family;
— your job;
— your ministry.

Does that mean that if there is a family problem, you don't go to work that day? Or if you have not had a quiet time that day, does it mean that you do not lead a Bible study? No. It means that over a period of days or weeks, the priorities are kept. There may be brief periods when one aspect (such as the job) jumps to the top and we concentrate almost totally on it.

Specifically, your priorities should come from your objectives. If an objective involves time with the family, then it must take a clear priority in the week. Daily or weekly, jot down your priorities. Base your decisions and weekly schedule on these priorities. It sounds simple. It is. And it works. Remember that you are working with those 36½ discretionary hours.

How do you go about scheduling your time to get everything done? This is the easiest process of all. The 3x5 card is the best time-management tool since the clock. On one side of the card, write your priorities for the week; on the other side, keep a running "do list" for each day of the week. Also, keep a list of small or quick items that you can do in a three-minute period or on the backstroke. (See figure 2.)

After making the "do list," order the activities according to priority. Some must be done simply from urgency, but if that becomes the norm, you are not adequately planning ahead.

We can follow the same procedure at work if we have a kind of job in which we have options on our time.

Front Side

Back Side

Do

Mow lawn
4. Finish Bible Study (Wed)
1. Work on testimony (2 hours)
   Write the Smiths
2. Talk to Kathy about schoolwork
3. Help Karen with math

Call / Misc.

1. Get Gas for Car
2. Call Jack 562-1173
3. Call Bob (during coffee break)

Priorities

1. Personal Quiet Time (15 min)
2. Talk with my wife 15 min. daily. Be available to the children.
3. Finish yard work
4. Work on my written personal testimony

Figure 2

To demonstrate the need for scheduling and planning, keep a record for a week of how you use your "off the job" time. Better yet, reflect on last week and write down how each evening and the weekend were used. What percentage of time was wasted?

A final suggestion: Because most of us work better with some regularity or habit, try to set up some kind of schedule. Do not try to do it by the minute, but in general terms. For example:

Monday	Open
Tuesday	Personal Bible study
Wednesday	Family night
Thursday	Group Bible study
Friday	Open for entertaining
Saturday	Morning: study and personal projects
	Afternoon: shopping and household projects
	Evening: open
Sunday	Morning: church
	Afternoon: plan week, extra time in prayer, special time with one of the children.

From this general schedule, plan the specifics for each week. Plan for interruptions and broken schedules by leaving some open or overflow time: you will need it. In planning like this, some worry about being "too organized" or "inflexible." Frankly, that problem is rare.

Discussion Questions

1. What is materialism? Give some specific evidences.
2. What is the definition of a biblical disciple?
3. What are key elements of witnessing on your job?
4. Are objectives a biblical or human concept?
5. Discuss the difference between objectives and activities.
6. Discuss the difference between priorities for today and priorities for a month. Will they be the same?
7. How can you make a schedule flexible?

8. Write out three sample objectives and discuss whether they are realistic and attainable.
9. Why do most people avoid setting objectives and scheduling?
10. Is it sin not to set objectives, priorities, or schedules? Explain your answer.
11. Discuss practical actions that have helped you to get more done in less time.
12. What are the major objectives for every Christian?
13. What place should outside ministry have in a person's objectives?
14. What should a Christian sacrifice for the sake of the family?

CHAPTER 4

GETTING AHEAD — NO MATTER WHAT

IT WAS Gary's first day on the job. His reputation as a brilliant scientist and an up-and-coming manager had preceded him. He was friendly to everyone and rapidly made the rounds to get to know his departmental personnel. But after several weeks it became clear that he found the right people to talk to and work with. He developed friendships with those who could serve him or aid his reputation. His ego and ambitions came first. And he was successful. He was soon assigned to choice projects where he even recruited some of his old "friends" to work for him. But instead of finding the friendly Gary they once knew, they now found a man with power and influence who was simply using them.

The Dilemma of Ambition

We can easily picture the classic ambitious man in our minds. He gets ahead by any means. He claws his way to the top. He disregards those who get hurt in his reach for success. He is pleasant when it serves his purpose and indifferent when he is not served. Though much of what he does helps the company or organization, we sense that his motive is totally self-serving. His goal may be position, money, or power.

Not only is this man trying to be president of the company, but he is also the factory worker trying to be foreman. He is the Christian trying to run the committee. She may be the wife pushing her husband and striving for status among women. He may be the clerk moonlighting at another job to make more money. He may be the father trying to direct his children's lives to achieve success vicariously through them.

Does that sound wrong? Of course it does. It *is* wrong. But if ambition is wrong, should we seek to remove all ambition? Let us look at ambition's opposite.

Joe Ambitionless. We know him, too. His house and yard are a mess. He sits and watches TV for hours every night. He never initiates family activities. His children run wild without discipline or direction. As a Christian he is a classic pew-sitter — doctrinally straight but totally uninvolved. He never accepts a responsibility by choice. In his job he is concerned only about security and adequate money. Is this the Christian standard? Of course not!

That is the dilemma. Too much ambition leads to presumptuous self-promotion. Too little ambition displays laziness and slothfulness. How much is too much? How much is too little?

Ambition itself is neither bad nor good. It is a part of our nature, like hunger, desire, or love. But hunger can become gluttony; desire can become craving; love can become lust. And ambition can become selfishness and pride. Like any normal drive, it can be misdirected.

The Bible does not condemn ambition, but it does condemn wrong *motives* prompting ambition, such as selfishness, pride, or greed. It does not condemn lack of ambition, but it may condemn the lack of faith and obedience. If the Scriptures lean in either direction, it is to encourage godly ambition. "Make it your ambition to lead a quiet life" (1 Thess. 4:11). Paul's ambition was to "press on toward the goal for the prize of the upward call of God in Christ Jesus" (Phil. 3:14) and to "know Him, and the power of His resurrection" (Phil. 3:10). Jesus preached the ambition to serve. "If any one wants to be first, he shall be last of all, and servant of all" (Mark 9:35).

We must be more specific to understand this in the biblical context. A dictionary definition of *ambition* is "(1) strong desire to gain a particular objective, specifically the drive to succeed, or to gain fame, power, wealth, etc.; (2) the objectives strongly desired." Therefore the right use of ambition depends on —

— the rightness of the goal;

— the rightness of the motive for reaching that goal.

"Whatever you do, do your work heartily, as for the Lord rather than for men; knowing that from the Lord you will receive the reward of the inheritance. It is the Lord Christ whom you serve" (Col. 3:23,24). This passage is packed with meaning for the working person. The only legitimate goal is to serve Christ. If we have serving Christ as our motive, the matter of promotion or raises can be left in God's hand. When a person works enthusiastically, he will usually produce more than the rest of the workers. In fact, working heartily may be interpreted as a striving for advancement by co-workers. Everyone agrees with the ideal of serving Christ, but in practice it can be difficult to discern when the motive is actually right.

Evidence of Unhealthy Ambition

Ambition can be misused. The problem is how to identify when ambition becomes sin. Here are a few indicators of unhealthy ambition:

Serving your own ego. "But you, are you seeking great things for yourself? Do not seek them" (Jer. 45:5). God has no place for the Christian on an ego trip. Such a person desires to be recognized, honored, and deferred to. He is self-serving and self-centered. He often thinks, "I wonder if they saw me do that?" or "Does he know *who* I am?" or "If I were in that position, they would listen to me!" Ambition focused on personal ego will not have God's blessing.

Grasping for position and power. "But Jesus called them to Himself, and said, 'You know that the rulers of the Gentiles lord it over them, and their great men exercise authority over

them. It is not so among you . . .' " (Matt. 20:25,26). The King
James Version reads, "But it shall not be so among you." The
world clutches for power and authority, exercising these for
personal benefit. Jesus condemns this motive. The Christian's
driving force cannot be a desire for position and power. If God
gives it, fine, but that is not to be the *end* goal. Guard against
the desire for authority. Even in churches, misplaced ambition
and grasping for leadership lead to conflicts and separations.
"But it shall *not* be so among you."

A desire to control others. "The rulers of the Gentiles *lord*
it over them, and . . . *exercise* authority . . ." (Matt. 20:25). The
world's pattern is to control people for personal goals. And
Christians, too, experience an inner urge to direct others, to
change their thinking, and to manipulate them. The tendency
is to control instead of influence. As this desire creeps forward,
know that it has crossed the line from godly to unhealthy
ambition.

A motive to be rich. "Do not weary yourself to gain
wealth, cease from your consideration of it. When you set your
eyes on it, it is gone. For wealth certainly makes itself wings,
like an eagle that flies toward the heavens" (Prov. 23:4,5). Or,
"Labour not to be rich" (KJV). "He who loves money will not be
satisfied with money, nor he who loves abundance with its
income. This too is vanity" (Eccl. 5:10). The Bible discusses
riches and possessions at great length. The Bible clearly
teaches that money is not evil, but that "the *love* of money is a
root of all sorts of evil, and some by longing for it have wan-
dered away from the faith, and pierced themselves with many a
pang" (1 Tim. 6:10).

A friend of mine has stated that his goal is to be independently wealthy. This intention has consumed him for years.
Today he is discontent, has family difficulties, and still is not
independently wealthy. Ambition for riches will not be blessed
by God. It is not a legitimate goal for a Christian.

But let us discuss this a little further. In our culture with
its prevailing focus on money and possessions, how can a
Christian discern what is healthy? Wealth per se is not sinful.
Hard work for more money is not sinful. The key is *why* we
want more money. Proper reasons such as food for the family,

education for our children, giving to the poor, providing employment in a business, and giving to the Lord are completely honorable.

God has provided wealth to some Christians. They often give generously to the Lord's work. Often we excuse the wealthy by saying they were rich before they were Christians. But the Christian who is working hard and becoming wealthy may be regarded with envy or suspicion. God gives some the gifts and abilities to be successful investors and businessmen. This is a legitimate endeavor. The only requirement is that he be a giving, spiritual Christian, that his business practices are honest, that he is generous to the Lord and others, and that the motive of his heart is *not* simply to be wealthy. A good study of this matter is Christ's parables of the talents (Matt. 25:14-30; Luke 19:12-26).

Personal competition. "Do nothing from selfishness or empty conceit" (Phil. 2:3). In the Phillips version this verse reads, "Never act from motives of rivalry or personal vanity." Again, "Where jealousy and selfish ambition exist, there is disorder and every evil thing" (James 3:16). Most Americans thrive on competition. In some philosophies, winning is the only thing that counts.

I enjoy handball much more than jogging for my physical exercise, because handball is competitive. Competition produces extra adrenalin in the system and stimulates greater activity. Competition has many benefits, but also dangers; problems arise when simple competition becomes personal rivalry. When the goal changes from doing an excellent job to "beating out" another person, competition has become an unhealthy ambition. We should compete against a standard, not another person.

The world's emphasis on competition is aptly described by Adam Smith: "You could take away all the trophies and substitute plastic heads or whales' teeth. As long as there is a way to keep score they will play."[1] Misdirected competition among Christians is especially distasteful and destructive. "But if you bite and devour one another, take care lest you be consumed by one another" (Gal. 5:15). In your job, do your work well, but guard against personal competition as motivating force.

Evidence of Healthy Ambition

Healthy ambition is possible — even more, it is necessary. Each person must examine his heart motives before God, so any list of good or bad motives is inadequate. Yet, a few examples may be helpful.

The desire to serve God. "It is the Lord Christ whom you serve" (Col. 3:24). The ambition to serve Christ is the highest a person can have. When you "do your work heartily" (v. 23) with this motive, God will bless your life and your work. We serve Christ primarily by being obedient to His Word. But the Bible instructs us to work diligently and honestly as a witness to those around us. Therefore we should make it our *basic* ambition to serve Christ. We are where we are because He put us there.

To be a witness. Our witness is determined by the quality of our work and our attitude. A lazy person will not have the respect of non-Christians; they must see the scriptural principles of diligence and honesty demonstrated.

Therefore a desire for promotion, for skill improvement, and for personal recognition can be right *if* the basic motive is to be a witness for Jesus Christ. A good test for this motive is to ask, "Have I witnessed to my co-workers recently?" You must both work well *and* speak to others for them to know your motivations for good work.

> Let your light shine before men in such a way that they may see your good works and glorify your Father who is in heaven (Matt. 5:16).

> This should be your ambition: to live a quiet life, minding your own business and doing your own works; just as we told you before. As a result, people who are not Christians will trust and respect you (1 Thess. 4:11,12 TLB).

> Conduct yourselves with wisdom toward outsiders [non-Christians], making the most of the opportunity (Col. 4:5).

To influence society. When God told Abraham of His intention to destroy Sodom and Gomorrah, He said, "If I find in Sodom fifty righteous within the city, then I will spare the whole place on their account" (Gen. 18:26). Later God said He would spare it if ten were found (v. 32). Many times in the Old Testament, we see God using one man to influence an entire nation — not just the Abrahams, Davids, and Elijahs, but also the fearful Gideons, cowardly Jonahs, and faithful Calebs.

A Christian *can* influence society. Non-Christians often experience God's blessing because of the presence and influence of Christians. To a great extent America has been blessed because of Christians in the society. The presence of one Christian can change the language in an office, restrain others from sin, influence decisions for honesty, and change the character of a neighborhood or a town.

More than once I have had senior officers or bosses apologize for using foul language when it slipped out in my presence. In the military it is a custom to throw a party upon promotion — usually a cocktail party. Six associates and I were promoted to various ranks about the same time, and three of us were Christians. We presented the idea of hosting a prime rib dinner rather than a cocktail party. It was more expensive but all liked the idea. This was a creative alternative that influenced even a longstanding tradition.

An ambition to influence society is worthy. This may be a prompting motive for entering politics or joining the PTA, secular service clubs, or other community endeavors. In many of these activities, influence is greater if you are highly respected in your job and profession.

To be used by God. Elisha was a farmer, called to ministry by Elijah while he was plowing in the fields (1 Kings 19:19-21). After some time of serving Elijah (1 Kings 19:21; 2 Kings 3:11), he asked, "Please, let a double portion of your spirit be upon me" (2 Kings 2:9). The context makes it clear that he deeply wanted to be used by God.

Solomon prayed, "Give Thy servant an understanding heart to judge Thy people to discern between good and evil" (1 Kings 3:9). When Solomon prayed to be used by God to serve others, God also blessed him with riches and honor (v. 13).

In Colossians Paul specifically prayed for Christians to be "bearing fruit in every good work and increasing in the knowledge of God; strengthened with all power" (Col. 1:10,11). God will bless a deep desire to be used by Him. To be used in a particular place or way may require certain position, status, or education. Thus a goal that in itself could be selfish ambition can be legitimate if undergirded with the deep desire to be used by God. In 1961 I sensed that God was leading me to teach at the Air Force Academy, where I could minister to cadets. But to do this I needed to obtain a master's degree. I had no deep ambition to return to school, but I did so to allow God to send me to the Air Force Academy. Education or status was not the goal, but obeying God was.

To lead spiritually. "It is a trustworthy statement; if any man aspires to the office of overseer, it is a fine work he desires to do" (1 Tim. 3:1). To seek spiritual leadership and influence is commendable. However, the list of qualifications following 1 Timothy 3:1 must be met. If they are not met, a person may be "conceited and fall into the condemnation incurred by the devil" (v. 6). A good discussion of spiritual leadership can be found in Oswald Sanders's book *Spiritual Leadership* (Moody Press, 1967). Howard Butt expresses the motivation well: "If you believe in Christ, you lead to love, outside of Christ you love to lead."[2]

To best use your spiritual gift. "And since we have gifts that differ according to the grace given to us, let each exercise them accordingly" (Rom. 12:6). God has given us particular gifts and abilities, and we are responsible for developing and using them. It is worthy to aspire to be trained or to have a position to use a specific gift. Sometimes gifts will coincide with abilities needed in a secular job. Although we should discover and develop our gifts, we should beware of this one thing: I question whether we can discover and develop our gifts unless we are growing as disciples and are doing those things commanded for every Christian (such as studying the Word, witnessing, obeying). God is interested in our daily walk with Him first of all.

I was traveling in India while writing this chapter. In that context, much of this discussion seems ironic. The unemployment rate exceeds 50 percent in many parts of India. Indian students told me that only 40 or 50 percent of those with bachelor's degrees will obtain jobs immediately after college graduation; for those with master's degrees, about 60 percent will find work; with doctorates, 70 percent. The rest may spend three or four years trying to find a job, and then many will resort to changing their career fields.

Thus I wondered if any of these thoughts on "getting ahead" applied to Indian students. As I discussed this with a Christian student, I found that the same *motives* were there. He asked me whether it was wrong to desire a car or a house. Not necessarily a *nice* car or a *fancy* house — just *a* car and *a* house. Quite a difference in perspective, isn't it? The *motives* for ambition are the same in India as they are here.

In summary, we conclude that ambition in itself is neither bad nor good, but the motive behind ambition must be examined in the light of Scripture. We must return to the three key principles.

First, God is totally in charge of our present and our future, and He will promote, prosper, or place us as He pleases. "For promotion cometh neither from the east, nor from the west, nor from the south. But God is the judge: he putteth down one, and setteth up another" (Ps. 75:6,7 KJV).

Second, each person must personally search out God's will for each decision and ambition. No one can judge our motives; we are personally and completely responsible for our decisions. "So then do not be foolish, but understand what the will of the Lord is" (Eph. 5:17). However, we should not neglect to seek counsel from godly, mature Christians. "The way of a fool is right in his own eyes, but a wise man is he who listens to counsel" (Prov. 12:15).

Third, our worth does not depend on whether we have great or small ability, much or little position, great or small riches. We must remember this: "For who makes you different from anybody else, and what have you got that was not given to you? And if anything has been given to you, why boast of it as if you had achieved it yourself?" (1 Cor. 4:7 *Phillips*).

What Cost Promotion?

Howard walked out of the plant manager's office as if floating on air. He had just been offered a promotion to exactly the kind of job he had dreamed of for years. It would mean a raise in pay and a secure status in the company. The only catch was that he would have to move three times in two years and finally settle in a large eastern city: a small price for such a significant offer.

Then his heart sank. He thought of his eight-year-old son. John had a birth defect that required special training. The family had moved here specifically because that training was available.

Howard shared the news with his wife. She too had mixed emotions. She wanted the best both for him and for John. So they talked, prayed, and reviewed what God was doing in their lives. Howard had an excellent influence and testimony at the plant; two of his co-workers had received Christ, and he was helping them to grow. Howard's two older children, Susan and Rick, had found their niche in a group of Christian teen-agers at their church. In fact, Howard and his wife had come to the city five years ago as young, indifferent Christians. God had gotten their attention through John's problem, and they sought spiritual help in a local church. They found a strong, Bible-teaching ministry and a layman who helped them to grow personally.

The family reasoned that they could probably find similar circumstances in the other cities along with help for John, and Howard could perhaps be apart from the family for part of the training. But the more they prayed, the less peace they felt regarding the promotion. After three weeks of careful consideration and counseling, Howard decided to turn down the promotion even though it very likely meant no further opportunities would be offered. The cost of promotion was simply too much to pay.

A hard decision? Certainly. Foolish? Perhaps, but we must allow God to lead in every circumstance. There are times when the world's system and standards simply will not give guidance to a Christian.

What are you willing to sacrifice to get ahead in your job: your family? your ministry? your personal spiritual growth? In many decisions you will sacrifice one or more of these unless you weigh all the factors carefully.

Sameer Zahr was a Palestinian refugee living in Lebanon. He became a Christian through the witness of Navigator-trained Arabs. He was discipled while in the University of Beirut, where he received a degree in business administration. In his first day on a sales job in a Kuwait chemical firm, his employer told him, "Sameer, the first thing I want you to understand is, this job is to be your god. We require this of our men."

Sameer shot up a quick prayer, looked his new boss in the eye, and said, "Sorry, but I already have a God. But I'll make a bargain with you. I'll work for you, and if I can't sell more in giving this company my second best than anybody you've got here who has made the company his god, you can fire me." Sameer's employer was startled but agreed to the bargain.

It was not easy, but Sameer worked hard and put God first and the company second. His second was better than anyone else's first. Today he is in charge of all contract negotiations in all Asia for this firm. God clearly honored Sameer's decision on priorities.

God will honor you if you put Him first in every aspect of your life. "Seek first His kingdom and His righteousness; and all these things shall be added to you" (Matt. 6:33). Christ clearly demands first priority. If your job causes you to neglect your spiritual life, you are walking on dangerous ground.

Many jobs do demand a great deal of time and effort. As a Christian you have a responsibility to demonstrate loyalty to your employer. When there is extra work to be done, you should do your part. But when the job demands your life, the priority is too high.

When opportunity for promotion does occur, weigh carefully its effects on your life. I suggest that you consider these factors:

• Your ability. Can you handle the new job without excessive time?

• Your location. Will it require change? (The next chapter examines this topic in detail.)

• Your motive. Why do you want the promotion?

• Your family. What impact will it have on your family life? on individual family members?

• Your spiritual life. Will you be hindered in your personal growth?

• Your spiritual ministry. Will it increase or decrease your effectiveness for Christ?

Many a man has sacrificed his family for his career. He works excessive hours, brings work home, undertakes heavy social obligations, and focuses on advancement. Meanwhile his wife and children are neglected; the children are raised by his wife alone. Yes, they have all they need materially, but no father. As the children become teen-agers they begin to live their own lives. Drugs, rebellion, and resentment take control of them, and suddenly dad realizes that he gave his life to the wrong things. Now his career seems meaningless, but it is too late. The damage has been done.

The same thing can happen when a man uses all his extra time for church activities or ministry. If you add career to ministry, the family receives even less time. The Scriptures clearly teach that "no one can serve two masters, for either he will hate the one and love the other, or he will hold to one and despise the other. You cannot serve God and Mammon [riches]" (Matt. 6:24).

Then how much can I give to my job? Here are a few of the common problems to be considered:

Overwork and overambition. These problems are prevalent in jobs that do not have fixed hours. Some workers tend to drive themselves beyond their physical and emotional limits. A person may be in a job ill-suited to his personality and ability. One frequent error is to try to produce too much in too short a time — to be overly optimistic about what can be accomplished. Jobs that *regularly* require more than fifty hours a week will lead to difficulty in family and ministry.

I like my job too much. Some people enjoy their work so much that it is almost recreation for them. But such an obsession with work can lead to excessive time away from home and to resenting any other activities. In my first year in the Air Force, I was assigned to Cape Kennedy as a mission controller. That was during the heyday of space, and the job was tremendously interesting. I gave it everything I had — working late nights and occasionally all night. Coupled with many Christian activities, it meant that I left home before my son awoke and came home after he went to bed. This went on for two years of his life. I was clearly neglecting my family. God had to get my attention in a rather severe way. I then spent the next two years winning him back. This took an entire reorientation of my priorities.

If you are one who loves your work, guard your time well. Take extra precautions to spend time with your family and to have a spiritual outreach.

Pressure to produce. Many jobs carry a great deal of pressure — especially if there is a commission or a quota. This can drain both emotions and time if a person is not particularly capable in the job. In this instance, ask God for special ability to perform and be able to relax in the midst of pressure.

Jobs beyond your ability, training, or capacity. Each of us has limits, even in tasks for which we are trained or have experience. Our ability will have limits, or we may have some native ability but not the proper training. When we have both the ability and the training, we may not have the capacity (how much we can accomplish in a given time) for the job.

When you neither recognize your limits, nor admit them, nor take action, you may work excessive overtime to catch up or learn. Even then you may not do the job right or well. You should let your boss know when you are unable to do the work. In most cases he will appreciate your honesty, since he wants the work done well. If you remain silent, you will in effect be lying to your boss by allowing him to assume you are qualified. This does not mean that you should never take risks or stretch yourself in new areas, but it does mean you should be direct with your superiors and ask for the training or help you need. Certainly the boss does not want the backhoe digging up a gas line or a cost overrun due to incorrect bidding. Combine a "can do" spirit with good judgment and honesty.

How much can you give to a job? All the effort and quality rightfully expected of you to earn your wages — and a little more beyond that. When there is a *legitimate* need for a *short time,* give it all the extra time and effort necessary. Never fail your employer when he needs help. Be reliable in emergencies, but do not "sell your soul to the company store."

At one point in my career I was working in the Pentagon. Everyone arrived in the office early, before the general, and did not leave until he left, which was often well after working hours. There really wasn't extra work to do, and nothing significant was accomplished during that extra time. It was simply part of a system that had built up: be there when the general was there. I decided I would arrive and leave at the stated times unless there was a special need. I finished all my work in that period. However, I can recall that when we had a real need, I worked right on through the night to get the job done.

Are Laboring Jobs Demeaning?

"My brethren, do not hold your faith in our glorious Lord Jesus Christ with an attitude of personal favoritism. For if a man comes into your assembly with a gold ring and dressed in fine clothes, and there also comes in a poor man in dirty clothes, and you pay special attention to the one who is wearing the fine clothes, and say, 'You sit here in a good place,' and you say to the poor man, 'You stand over there, or sit down by my footstool;' have you not made distinctions among yourselves, and become judges with evil motives?" (James 2:1-4).

Little has changed in the nineteen centuries since those words were written. In Christian circles there is still a strong tendency to value or give honor to the person of position or wealth. When describing a group or church you often hear of "Dr. Jones" or "Mr. Johnson, the president of the firm" or "Colonel Jackson." Seldom is it combined with "Mr. Williams, the carpenter [unless he owns a business]" or "Mr. Benton, the mechanic." Perhaps without really meaning to, we place extra value on those who have position or wealth or marks of notable success.

The truth is, churches, neighborhoods, and social groups *do* divide along class, social, and economic lines. If a church is large, it tends to subdivide into smaller, homogeneous groups. Usually a person finds himself in the social or economic group directly related to his kind of job. Is this wrong? Are not all Christians to be equal in the body of Christ? Yes, but remember that society is not Christian and that God intends for us to reach out to all society.

If every person who became a Christian were suddenly famous or rich, would that person continue to live in that old house, eat the same food, and drive the same car? Or would he rent or buy a nicer house, wear better clothes, and even change social associations? Most would do the latter. Recall the earlier discussion on concepts of witness: God's objective is to influence and reach all segments of the community. Therefore He has sovereignly placed Christians in every level of society, with different abilities and social and economic standing — to be witnesses.

Laboring and unskilled jobs. There is no truly "unskilled" job: every task involves skill. Many people could not endure a job requiring great physical strength or stamina; some professionally trained persons are totally incompetent when it comes to manual skills.

I read recently of a man who bought a new gadget — unassembled, of course. After reading and rereading the instructions, he could not understand how it went together. Finally he sought the help of an old handyman who was working in the backyard. The old fellow picked up the pieces, studied them, and then began assembling the gadget. In a short time he had it all put together.

"That's amazing!" said the man. "And you did it without even looking at the instructions!"

"Fact is," said the handyman, "I can't read. And when a fellow can't read, he's got to think."[3]

Jobs do require different degrees of mechanical skill, physical strength, and mental or academic ability. Wages are generally related to the supply of people who can do a particular job and the public demand for the service or product. Consider who would be missed most quickly: lawyers, engineers, and dentists; or garbage collectors, store clerks, and truckdrivers. Certainly the latter would be missed more quickly, but the former probably earn more money.

In Scripture, great honor is bestowed on persons with mechanical skills. The farmer or laborer who is diligent and faithful is exalted. Gideon was a farmer. Peter was a fisherman. God uses spiritual men regardless of their wealth or position. "For consider your calling, brethren, that there were not many wise according to the flesh, not many mighty, not many noble [whom God chose]" (1 Cor. 1:26).

God will certainly use the talented and wise man, but such a one is often too proud to open himself up to God. In history we see that many times God has used men of common background and ordinary occupations.

Are laboring or unskilled jobs demeaning? The answer is a resounding no! It is no biblically. It is no in terms of value to society. It is no in regard to human worth. It is no in the eyes of law. It is yes only in the warped value system of a materially corrupt society. A person's value is not in what he *does*, but in who he *is*.

Does this mean that a person should not attempt to gain more skills or education to get a higher-paying job? Should he placidly accept his lot in life and not try to change? Of course not. But it means that if his ability or training is such that change is unlikely or impossible, he must not be bitter against God for his station in life. God has placed him there for a specific purpose and clearly promises him peace and great contentment in his circumstances.

Recognition of personal ability. Are people really equal? Yes, they are of equal worth in God's sight. But they are not equal in ability or attainment. People have widely varied abilities, manual skills, intellectual capacities, and spiritual gifts. "Since we have gifts that *differ* according to the grace given to us . . ." we read in Romans 12:6. Each of us is different and unique in God's sight. We must recognize that some are more intelligent or more skillful. It is not a matter of "better or worse," just difference.

Recognize also that people with essentially equal ability will have different levels of attainment. Even among David's mighty men, Benaiah "was honored among the thirty, but he *did not attain* to the three" (1 Chron. 11:25). God simply wants each one to use to the fullest the abilities He has given. The end result is up to Him.

It is easy to be jealous of another Christian who has great gifts and abilities. And that Christian may be jealous of someone else. We read earlier, "Where jealousy and selfish ambition exist, there is disorder and every evil thing" (James 3:16). This is another form of coveting what belongs to another, and it is sin.

What about equality in the Christian community? Everyone must be treated as equal in value and we must not show preference to any (James 2:1-4). But even in this there are differing gifts and abilities to fulfill the total functioning of the body of Christ. We *must* recognize these differences. Not everyone is a leader; not everyone can sing; not everyone can teach. Assuming that the spiritual qualifications of 1 Timothy 3 are met, not every person is qualified for every responsibility or office in the church. One who cannot balance his own checkbook or prepare a budget for his family should not be church treasurer. A person who effectively teaches a class of eight may not be able to teach a class of fifty.

We need to recognize abilities and help people find their most productive place in the body of Christ. Remember, too, that we all change: God changes us as we grow. We can learn new skills and develop our gifts and abilities, so we must never restrict ourselves or others with a "permanent" evaluation.

A proper self-image. Many Christians have a distorted view of themselves. They do not see themselves as others see them, nor do they see themselves as God sees them. In some respects they feel inferior; in some, superior. "I say to every man among you not to think more highly of himself than he ought to think; but to think so as to have sound judgment" (Rom. 12:3). The Phillips version says, "Try to have a sane estimate of your capabilities." And in the Living Bible, "Be honest in your estimate of yourselves."

What we seek is truth about ourselves. But truth often hurts. We would rather live in a dream world imagining that we are this or that. One of the marks of a mature Christian is that he welcomes truth in every aspect of life; he becomes more truthful to and about himself. A proper self-image is not an inflated ego, nor is it an attitude of worthlessness. It is a growing knowledge of gifts and abilities and a spirit of thanksgiving that God has made you as you are. It is not an "I-guess-that's-the-way-I-am" attitude that suppresses change and hinders growth. It is a realistic evaluation that forms a basis for change and growth.

Here are some ideas for developing a good self-image and a "sane estimate" of your attitudes:

1. Ask God to enable you to see the abilities and gifts He has given you and to be thankful for them.

2. List your strengths, weaknesses, and abilities as you know them. (Consider in what ways God has blessed you in the past.)

3. Ask two or three close friends and possibly your employer to evaluate you in these aspects.

4. When you feel you have clearly identified a particular strength, weakness, or ability, consciously thank God for what you have *and* for what you do not have.

5. Begin to use and develop your strengths and abilities.

6. Begin to withdraw from activities or tasks for which you are clearly not gifted.

A friend of mine was discussing the future with a sixty-two-year-old widow. The widow said, "I was born to be somebody." She had a sense of destiny, not despair. You were born to be somebody. God has that special purpose for your life.

Should everyone be a professional? At times it seems that there is pressure on every teen-ager to go to college and become a professional person — a doctor, engineer, teacher, or social worker. But on the basis of gifts and abilities, not everyone should do this. In fact, not everyone who *can* do it necessarily *should*. Many people are unhappy in an office or a high-pressure professional environment. There are many in high-paying professions only because they were trained for it and are well-paid. They would really like to farm, work in construction, or other fields in which a college education is unnecessary. For a Christian, a job means evaluating not only what he *can* do, but what he *likes* to do and ultimately what God *calls* him to do.

A good friend of mine was highly trained in a complex scientific field. He was successful and competent. Yet he frequently expressed a desire to do something he both enjoyed and excelled in — carpentry.

Don't let the world press you into doing what does not fit your gifts *and* your emotional bent.

How to Be Fulfilled in Your Job

Everyone wants to be fulfilled in his job. But can you know when you are fulfilled? Is it when you are getting enough money? when you are free from conflicts or problems on the job? when you have job security? when you feel "good" and are happy about your circumstances?

Certainly it is not just one of these things, nor is it all of them combined. You can be totally fulfilled in the midst of conflict and problems. Contribution brings fulfillment even when pay and other benefits are small. You would deny your humanity to expect total, irrevocable fulfillment. Fulfillment is dynamic and changing. You must look at it like climate, not the weather: weather is the daily situation of varying conditions; climate is the average weather in a given area. Look at the average fulfillment over a period of time.

Measuring fulfillment is difficult. In fact, job fulfillment cannot be measured in terms of the job alone. It *must* be measured in concert with your personal and family satisfaction and circumstances. The following questions provide an approximate gauge for job fulfillment:

1. To the best of your understanding, do you have a vital daily walk with Christ? (Personal devotions, obedience in major areas of your life.)

    Yes   No

2. Do you function in your family according to the pattern of Scripture? (Husband and wife fulfilling biblical roles, family guided on a spiritual basis in love and unity.)

    Yes   No

3. Are you basically happy with your job?

    Yes   No

4. Do you do your best on the job?

    Yes   No

5. Have you witnessed to someone on your job in the last year?

    Yes   No

6. Has it been at least six months since you sincerely contemplated quitting your job?

    Yes   No

7. Do you feel the job you are doing is worthwhile?

    Yes   No

8. Do you feel the job adequately makes use of your abilities?

    Yes   No

9. Do you go to work daily with ease of mind? (As opposed to dreading it or focusing mostly on the weekend.)

    Yes   No

10. Does your job meet the primary financial needs of your family?

    Yes   No

Clearly there is no "right" score. But if you answered no to question 1 or 2, you probably do not find peace in your job. If you responded yes to five or more of the remaining eight, you are reasonably fulfilled in your job now.

Before we set forth a few suggestions for increasing job fulfillment, consider a basic question: Does God intend that every person be fulfilled in his job?

Is it sin not to be fulfilled? Biblically the answer must be no. God does not promise or command job fulfillment. We must be *content* in our circumstances, but we might not experience *fulfillment*. The Bible does not say directly that God does not expect a person to be fulfilled in the job, but this is derived inductively from passages like Colossians 3:22,23. This statement was specifically addressed to slaves: they were to work heartily as to the Lord. Being a slave was not a fulfilling job, but one was to be content as a Christian. In prison, Joseph was not fulfilled, but he was content (Gen. 39–41). Does God expect a man who spends his days in a coal mine breathing dust and working hard to say he wants to do this more than anything else? Working on an assembly line, putting the same part on a car or punching out the same machine part every day, may not be your idea of an ideal job. Many jobs are difficult, offer little recognition, and allow no prospects of promotion. In such circumstances we must accept God's sovereignty in placing us where we are. Biblical fulfillment is found, not only on the job, but in the interrelationship of personal activities, family ties, and work. Many jobs serve the family by providing for them. In fact, Christians will rarely find real fulfillment only in a job.

But is it legitimate to strive for fulfillment? Yes, it is. Here are five key steps to work on:

1. Acknowledge that God has placed you in your job and thank Him for it.

2. Do the best work you can in your job, both in attitude and action.

3. Do whatever is necessary to resolve personal conflicts with co-workers even if it means losing face.

4. Actively seek and take advantage of opportunities to witness to those with whom you work.

5. Begin a program of development to improve or change jobs if this is within your abilities and desires.

These are simple suggestions, but effective when you put them into practice.

Discussion Questions

1. How do you recognize ambition in your life?
2. How much can you legitimately give to your job?
3. Should everyone try to qualify for professional or higher-paying jobs?
4. How do you explain the obvious distinctions between ability and gifts?
5. What is fulfillment in life? In a job? In marriage?
6. Discuss the statement "Not everyone can expect to be fulfilled in his job."
7. Are some jobs of less value to God and society than others?
8. How much emphasis should a Christian put on promotion and pay?

CHAPTER 5

PULLING UP ROOTS

THE DRIVE home from the plant that night seemed to take hours instead of thirty minutes. Phil's heart was pounding, and he felt as if someone had just punched him in the stomach. He was laid off. He had thought his job was totally secure. He knew he was one of the most competent men in his job. But so were a thousand other men who were also laid off that day.

There began months of searching for work. When the first shock was over, he settled down to a serious search for work in the same city. Soon his determination turned to panic. Nothing was available. He began looking in other locations. Then he heard that he could have a job in a city one thousand miles away. He should have been happy, but he had to decide whether he was willing to pull up roots and move his family. He had lived there fifteen years. He thought of his children — their friends, school, and church. The adjustments could be especially great for his teen-agers.

We live in a mobile society. Families in metropolitan areas move an average of every four or five years; few children go to school in the same city from kindergarten through high school graduation. The process of moving often causes the children to suffer.

Factors to Consider in Change

What factors should you consider in making a move or in changing jobs? I will mention only four, though many others could be included. Each is dealt with more fully later in this chapter.

Family. Without question, the children suffer the most from a move. They lose their friends, teachers, familiar surroundings, and key extracurricular activities. Adults frequently underestimate the emotional impact a major change has on a child. The older the child, the more difficult the adjustment to new surroundings, for he makes new friends less easily. Months pass before he is thoroughly integrated into a new church or school situation. Children do not direct our lives, but they deserve *consideration* in any decision.

Who *really* bears the major work in a move? The wife. Yes, husbands, we may do some packing, load, and unload the goods. But who cleans the house to sell, does most of the packing, disengages the children from school, unpacks, lives (and even cooks) out of suitcases in the temporary apartment, cleans the new house, and all the while cares for the children and their needs? Your wives. We finish our job, load and unload the furniture, help find the house, and then immerse ourselves in the new job. This may not be all bad, but we must face the facts and understand their implications.

A number of years ago my wife had a baby, typed my master's thesis, and made two major moves — all in six months. At the same time I undertook significant ministry that included activities with students in our home. Neither of us realized the physical impact on Mary until almost a year later. Then, for almost a year, we had to reduce our activities until her full strength returned. We learned a valuable lesson.

In any decision to "pull up roots," your family deserves prime consideration.

Church and spiritual involvement. Life is a spiritual involvement: everyone receives and gives. You must ask, "Why did God put me here in the first place? Is this mission accomplished?" Vital spiritual nourishment provides the foundation for your spiritual growth. You need the church. You need the fellowship of the body of Christ. If you and your family are receiving deep spiritual feeding, you will want to consider carefully before leaving it. If you leave, what spiritual environment exists where you are going? Have you investigated it? How mature are you — can you survive spiritually where there is little spiritual fellowship?

Besides taking in spiritual food, you also should be giving spiritually to others. What is your ministry now, and what opportunities exist in the new location? By the term *ministry* I mean not just organizational functions like teaching Sunday school or serving on a church board, but also outreach to people in the job and neighborhood. Unless you have trained another Christian to replace you where you are, there will be no one to carry on your work.

Your job. Are you realistic about the demands of your new job? Will it meet your expectations? Will it consume your time? Depending on why you changed or moved, your new job may cause more problems than it solves. Motives — both good and bad — for changing jobs will be discussed in the next two sections.

God's will. Ultimately you must ascertain God's will for you. No set of rules or guidelines will ever "tell" you what to do. When all the counsel and tests are in, you must find yourself on your knees seeking that final word from God. God longs for the best for you, so take the time and effort to discern His will — and then do it. A brief summary of this subject is provided later in this chapter.

Valid Reasons for Change

God directed Moses to leave Egypt for the desert, to return to Egypt, and finally to lead the nation of Israel out of Egypt to the Promised Land. God led David through adversity to live in many places, from caves to palaces. God led Paul on his missionary journeys. Move and change are not sinful; God continually directs us to various places of ministry and work.

But when there is a choice, we must consider our real motives for change — and there are good ones. Some we choose, and some God forces on us.

Family. Again? Yes, the family again — first. A friend of mine took a high-paying, prestigious job in another part of the country. He and his wife agreed on a two-year testing period because they had some reservations on the advisability of the move for the family. Neither his wife nor his children ever adjusted to the new environment and relationships. They were not sullen and complaining, but that settled peace was missing. After two years they moved back to their original location with no real guarantee of a job. He did find a job, and the family's happiness was restored.

On the other hand, a time may come when teen-age associations need to be severed. Al and Ginger had two teen-agers and one pre-teen. Their city was becoming a center of drugs and student unrest. Though Christians, their two teen-agers began to develop relationships and undergo pressures that were deeply affecting their thinking, attitudes, and actions. Although Al's job was rewarding and promised advancement, he decided to move to another city to change his children's environment.

Pay careful attention to your family's needs. You cannot rebuild past years in their lives.

Here are a number of family reasons that enter into a decision to move:

- Health problems of one family member;

- Schooling for the children;

- A frantic family activity cycle that cannot easily be changed in your current location;

- Company pressures and demands that are hurtful to the family.

Your company moves you. If you work for a large company that has several locations, the possibility of a move always exists. The company might ask you to move, or economic conditions may reduce work at one plant and confront you with the choice of moving or quitting. You don't *have* to move, yet the economics of the situation may force you to move. It could be a big step of faith to stay and trust God for another job. If you choose to stay, you would want to know clearly that it was God's will, since employment opportunities elsewhere are often uncertain. When you have a choice, seek God's will with your family in your current circumstances.

Personal satisfaction and a new job. The challenge and excitement of a new job motivate many people. A new job can offer the way out of difficult working conditions or an unstable financial situation.

Marty Harris had worked on construction jobs since he was eighteen. The work was seasonal, financially unstable, and left him dissatisfied. At age twenty-three he decided to begin training for other work. For six years, the family scrimped and restricted its schedule so that he could attend technical school at night. He finally graduated, but there were no job opportunities in his city. After twenty-nine years in one place, three children with deep ties in school and the neighborhood, and a good church situation, a major move appeared to be the only way to break into the new field. After much prayer, Marty and his wife decided that God wanted them to move. The major issues in their decision centered around Marty's personal satisfaction in the job and security for the family. They were not running from anything: he had been well-respected in the construction business.

As Christians we don't operate on the myth that "what is hard is good" or "the opposite of what I want is what God wants." God wants to give us the desires of our hearts and to give us peace and happiness. If we attempt to work in fields in which we lack ability or gifts, personal dissatisfaction soon surfaces. Dissatisfaction often provides a clue that a change could be needed, *provided* our relationship with God is secure and we are not seeking escape from problems.

A new job in a new location can stimulate new ministry opportunities, new contacts for witness, new growth by stepping out in faith, and renewed motivation in your job. God opens as well as closes doors. The open door may be a new job and a move.

Changing jobs without changing location can provide new job opportunities or satisfaction without a major disruption of family and church circumstances. Make that possibility a first consideration when you contemplate a change of jobs.

Health. When one member of the family has a significant health problem, you have a clear responsibility to do whatever is necessary to help. A change of climate may be recommended by a doctor for asthma, hay fever, or other illnesses. In many places, expert medical facilities for particular problems are not available within reasonable distances. Sometimes a particular job can cause specific health problems.

Remember that many health problems have an emotional base. Such difficulties are every bit as real as a broken leg or a case of flu. Although I hesitate to recommend a change of job or location *only* because of emotional health, we should recognize that location, financial circumstances, the type of job, and church relationships *do* have a profound effect on our emotional health. A different location or job can be restorative *if* the roots of the problem have also been treated.

Opportunities for ministry. As a person matures in his Christian life, he begins to develop a new view of his spiritual needs, gifts, and contributions. Economic achievement and worldly success lose their glitter. Reality shatters unfulfilled dreams.

An old man brought a painting to a famous painter who asked, "Who painted this?"

The old man replied, "A twelve-year-old boy."

Excitedly the famous painter said, "Bring him to me and I'll make him the greatest artist the world has ever known."

"That's impossible," said the old man. "I'm the boy."

Life is more than work and money. God plans that you make a particular spiritual contribution, but you need to prepare and train for it. However, opportunity for training can be lost. You also must be in the right place. Would you be willing to move in order to get help in your personal life so that you can more effectively minister to others? Are you willing to invest a few years now to be ready for your contribution to the body of Christ later? I am not talking about full-time Christian work, but rather about being an effective layman in a secular job. If you find a church or a person who can help you prepare to make an effective *contribution*, seize that opportunity.

God can also lead you to move or to change jobs to involve yourself in a particular ministry or outreach. As a young Air Force officer, I was assigned to an exciting job at Cape Kennedy. Through a series of circumstances, God brought the Air Force Academy to my attention. I began to consider the opportunities to witness and minister to students there. Ministry to cadets by outside groups was discouraged, so an inside influence was needed. I began to pray and prepare. I received counsel that the academy was not the best assignment for my career, but I sensed God's leading. After three years of preparation, God led me to a position on the faculty. As a result, several hundred cadets have come to know Christ there and are now vibrant Christian Air Force officers.

Has God been speaking to you about a particular place of ministry?

A new start. We read frequently of people who make drastic changes in their careers: the engineer who becomes a farmer; the carpenter who goes to college and becomes a doctor; the independent businessman who gets fed up with the pressure and takes a job with hourly pay. Many people do not make the right career choices at first. Should they just accept it as "fate" and "gut" it out for life? Not necessarily. God can lead such a person to a new life and career.

Sam was thirty-one, married with three children, active in Christian endeavors, had one year of college, and held a well-paying job as a janitor. God led him to return to school and prepare to be a teacher, even though he would initially be paid less. He attended night school for the next seven years. It was difficult for him and the family, but they were sure of their direction. At age thirty-eight he graduated from the university and began a teaching career.

If you became a Christian as an adult or have recently gained new maturity in your Christian life, you may be in circumstances that are too complicated and difficult to restore to bring fulfillment. You may need to make a new start by moving or changing jobs. Allow God to change you and your situation if that is the case.

This chapter so far has dealt chiefly with reasons for job changes within our control. But what about when we have been laid off or fired?

Laid off. Whenever the national economy changes and possibly deteriorates, increasing numbers of people may be out of work. The illustration that opens this chapter points up the dilemma many face in such a circumstance.

A friend of ours, an engineer, was suddenly laid off. He had thought his job secure, so the layoff was completely unexpected. He anticipated no problem in getting another job but soon found that nothing was available anywhere in the country. Finally, as a step of faith and after much prayer, he and his family sold their house and took their savings, and he went back to graduate school to qualify for work in a different field. During the months of job-hunting, the family was quickly enlightened about the status of the unemployed. Even in their church relationships, people rarely offered help or inquired about their needs.

Writing on this subject in *Eternity* magazine, Sara Welles said, "Our friends at church either smiled weakly or avoided us. I remarked to my husband that it was almost as though one of us had died. People acted afraid or embarrassed."[1]

Being without work is frightening and unnerving. It hurts our pride and drives us to God. It certainly provides a legitimate reason for a move. But what do you do when you lose your job? Here are some practical suggestions:

1. As hard as it may be, thank God for your circumstances.
2. With your wife, list some lessons God may want you to learn in this circumstance.
3. Take a financial inventory: What are your savings? How much unemployment compensation can you draw, and for how long? What insurance policies do you have with cash value for a loan? What do you have that can be quickly converted to cash if necessary — e.g., a second car or a recreational vehicle? Avoid borrowing money at interest.
4. From this financial inventory, determine how long you can be without work and still subsist.
5. Work out a severely reduced budget. Cut all frills. You can probably live on a half or two-thirds of your previous income. Do *not* use credit cards. If you have heavy debts with high time payments, try to make a reduced payment and write to your creditor explaining your situation.
6. Discuss your situation with your family. Pray together.

They will rally together and be willing to live on less.

    7. Let your pastor know your circumstances, and ask the church to pray. Tell your friends: they may know of other employment.

    8. Don't be too proud to accept food gifts or other offers of help. Allow others to have the joy of sharing, but don't expect it as your "right."

    9. Inform your out-of-town friends and relatives that you are seeking a job. They may know of opportunities.

    10. Immediately begin to seek work. If a résumé of experience would be helpful, begin writing a *good* resume. The local library has books to help you. If you are a poor writer, ask a friend to assist you.

    11. Apply for unemployment benefits. You and your company have paid for these benefits: they are not a handout.

    12. Plan to put in eight-hour days in job-hunting. That is your "job" now. Send your résumé to out-of-town employers early, since it will take time for them to reply.

    13. Always seek a personal interview with the one responsible for the hiring.

    14. In the process of job-hunting, you will usually find some poor, low-paying jobs not in your field. Keep a list of these. You may need to take such a job temporarily. In fact, if this kind of job is available at night or part-time, take it. You can continue to hunt for a better job during the day.

    15. Consult an employment service.

    16. Consider the possibility of retraining or schooling. This may be your opportunity to change fields.

    17. Consider the possibility of your wife's working temporarily. Although this is not ideal, it must be considered an option.

    18. If work is not available locally, think seriously of changing locations.

    19. Above all, improve your personal walk with God. He may be trying to get your attention.

    I also recommend reading the book *What Color is Your Parachute? — A Practical Manual for Job Hunters and Career Changers*, by Richard Nelson Bolles.[2]

    "You are fired." The words "You're fired!" bring chills. When it happens, it seldom seems justified to the employee.

But it does happen. Whether the reasons were valid or not, he cannot change the fact. He is without work, and the fact of being fired is on his employment record.

It may be helpful to know some of the major reasons people are fired.

- Poor work performance (quality, speed, or production);
- Job beyond a person's ability or training (unqualified);
- Bad relationships with others (conflicts);
- Making serious errors on the job;
- Laziness or intentionally slow work;
- Undependability.

When you are fired, you can follow essentially the same suggestions given in the previous section. There are these additional comments, however: first, a warning. You may have been "fired" even though the terminology used was "laid off." Usually you know when that is the case. If this was your situation, you must admit it or else you will not learn the lesson God has for you in the experience — and you will repeat the mistake in your next job.

1. First you must determine why you were fired. (Rarely is the reason your Christian witness.)
   a. Write down the reason your former employer gave for your dismissal. If you are unsure, call and ask him. Ask for the straight truth.
   b. Write down the reason you think you were fired. Be honest with yourself. Try to trace the problem to its source.
   c. Determine how you can prevent this from happening again.
2. Be honest with your prospective employers.
3. Guard against bitterness in your life.

Now follow the guidelines stated in the previous section. Remember that no failure is final. Good performance on the next job will erase the stigma of being fired.

Questionable Reasons for Change

Just as there are valid reasons for changing a job or location, there are also questionable reasons for changing. Several of these reasons, mentioned earlier, bear repeating in this context.

Money. Money would be *a* reason for a change, but seldom should be *the* reason. If you live at or below the subsistence level, a change for more money is valid. If you change just to get more money for more material things, that is questionable.

Career climbing. Be cautious about changing jobs or locations to advance in your career. This reason must coincide with careful considerations of the family's needs and other factors. One or two changes for career purposes could be acceptable, but frequent moves when your children are older can create problems. When the children are young, moves are less traumatic for the family.

Running from problems. If your problems are primarily of your own making, running away will not solve them. Do everything you can to solve them without a move.

The company says so. This by itself is not sufficient reason to move. It is only a factor. You can quit or take a lower-paying job in the company.

Too Late to Change

Is it ever too late to change job, career, or location? Ideally, we would like to say "never!" Realistically, limitations do exist. The three factors that must be considered are —

> — time and age;
> — finances;
> — family.

If you are in the late forties or older, age limits the feasibility of a new job or career. Many companies hesitate to hire people in that age bracket unless they have unusual qualifications or experience (e.g., an expert machinist or an executive). The ideal time for a career change is in the thirties. Then you know many of your own abilities and limitations and still have time to be productive for a company in your new career. Time is a factor in retraining and preparation for a new job. Some careers require several years of training, and others take only months.

The greatest barrier to career change is lack of finances. Most people simply do not have the money to tide them over a period of education or training. Many do not have enough to make a move for a new job. But if God's will is clear and your desire is great, it can be done. In cases of education and formal training, don't forget the GI bill as a source of financial aid if as a veteran you qualify. Student loans with low interest and liberal repayment terms are available. Much training and education can be obtained in night courses. You and your mate may need to work part-time for a couple of years. Without question, sacrifice will be involved. But sacrifice now is an investment for the future.

If you are contemplating a job change (not career change), begin a savings program and tighten the budget now. Often you must take a pay reduction to begin work in a different locale or company. But take warning not to be a job-hopper: employers are suspicious of frequent moves.

Since sacrifice of some kind often accompanies job and career changes, you must ascertain the total impact on your family. Is it fair to them? Do they support the change? Will it rob your children of their most valuable possession — you? Can your wife undergo the pressures resulting from your decision? Do not sacrifice your family for your personal gain or satisfaction. But take into account the possible future benefits the change may hold for them.

It is never too late to change, but the cost increases with time and age. You cannot always wait for things to be better — they probably won't be.

Guidelines for Finding God's Will

Everyone wants a magic formula for finding God's perfect will. We want one-two-three, no-fail instructions with a money-back guarantee. But there is no such thing. Walking by faith is the heart of the Christian life. And to walk by faith we must know God's will in small and large things. Yet knowing God's will and doing God's will are not the same. Knowing but not doing is sin; doing without knowing is folly.

God wants us to know His will: "So then do not be foolish, but understand what the will of the Lord is" (Eph. 5:17). God promised us guidance: "I will instruct you and teach you in the way which you should go; I will counsel you with My eye upon you. Do not be as the horse or as the mule which have no understanding, whose trappings include bit and bridle to hold them in check" (Ps. 32:8,9). Although an automatic formula does not exist, there are well-known and tried principles which will guide you in finding God's will.

A personal walk with God. Unless you are in a right relationship with God, trying to find His will in some major or minor decision is presumptuous. God has more basic things to communicate to you. If you are having difficulty determining His will, examine these prerequisites:

1. Are you a Christian? God responds only to His children. If you have never personally asked Jesus Christ to be your Savior, you cannot expect guidance from God (see John 3:16).

2. Have you confessed known sin? There may be factors in your life that God has been showing you for some time. "If I regard wickedness [sin] in my heart, the Lord will not hear" (Ps. 66:18). To clear the lines of communication, confess your sin to God (see 1 John 1:9).

3. Are you daily in fellowship with God? Do you have a daily time of Scripture reading and prayer? Would you go for days without listening or speaking to your mate? Similarly, God wants us to have daily communication with Him.

4. Are you obeying what you know? We are already aware of many things God wants us to do. These include —

> — vital fellowship with other believers in a church;
> — an open identification with Christ by your action and verbal witness;
> — a scriptural family relationship.

God may have shown you His will in the past and you refused to obey. Until you do what you already know of His will, you cannot expect guidance. The story of Israel in the Old Testament proves that they *knew* God's commands, *refused* to do them, and were *separated* from God's continued blessing — *until* they repented and began to obey (see Nehemiah 8 and 9 for an excellent summary on this point).

Pray. The next step is to pray. Put your heart in neutral and tell God you are willing to do whatever He directs. Ask to be made willing. Pray regularly about the details of your decisions, and ask for His guidance; pray with your family; ask others to pray (1 Peter 3:12; Matt. 7:7,8).

Use the Scriptures. As you read the Word regularly, ask God to impress on you statements or ideas that shed light on your motives, thinking, or decisions. Do not expect to be "told" by a Bible verse what you should do, nor turn automatically to passages that favor your desire. Simply ask God to use His Word and His Spirit to speak to you. Avoid jerking verses out of context and making them say things God never intended. Look for direct commands and principles (Heb. 4:12).

Examine circumstances. Get the facts. Write them down. In fact, at this point write down as much as you can from facts, Scriptures, and counsel. Words on paper are more objective than feelings and impressions.

Obtain godly counsel. Others can often see things we cannot. They ask questions that cause us to consider new directions. They may discern faulty thinking or even sin. For counsel involving spiritual matters, counsel only with Christians. "How blessed is the man who does not walk in the counsel of the wicked" (Ps. 1:1).

There are times, however, when it is proper to counsel with non-Christians. For example, in gathering data on a particular job, factual information about a city, or advice on your qualifications for a position, it would be in order to heed counsel of non-Christians. But when the spiritual dimension is needed, non-Christians can offer nothing. Be careful not to "stack" your counsel by going only to those you know will give counsel in a biased direction. Remember that no one can make a decision for you — and you must not expect anyone to do so. On highly emotional issues such as marriage, there is a tendency to seek counsel from various persons until you find someone who agrees with your desire and opinions. Carefully guard against that possibility (see Prov. 15:22).

Personal desire. Your personal desires are important. God wants you to be happy. If you are in fellowship with Him, your personal feelings and desires can be an indication of God's direction. Write down your personal inclination. On paper it may prove obviously emotional or strongly of the flesh. Written desires also help you to relate your personal feelings to the facts and circumstances (see Ps. 37:4).

Patience. We usually try to hurry God. Our byword is "now." God often says "wait." We want God's direction immediately, but growth and maturity are evidenced by willingness to wait on God (see Heb. 10:36; James 1:3,4; and Ps. 37:7).

Lorne Sanny, president of The Navigators, once told me, "There are good decisions and fast decisions, but there are no good, fast decisions." Yet there are occasions when time is essential. God is a God of perfect timing: He will give you direction when there is a deadline. But do not be forced into a hurried decision when there is excessive pressure and you do not have God's clear direction. Wait upon God.

Health. *Never* make a decision when you are ill, depressed, or fatigued. Never make a major decision when you are angry or emotionally upset.

Peace in your heart. "Let the peace of Christ rule [be the umpire or arbiter] in your hearts" (Col. 3:15). God gives a settled peace to those who do His will. It may not be the candy-sweet, good-feeling kind of peace you might sense when sitting in the sun on your day off. Nor will it be the euphoric excitement you feel after your team has won. You can have peace in the midst of fear — the solid assurance of knowing you are doing God's will.

When I began to consider returning to school for a Ph.D., I fought the idea. I did not want to go. I knew how much work was involved. I knew I risked failure. When I made the decision, I was apprehensive — but I knew it was what God wanted. I knew I was in God's will even in the turmoil of fear. Then I had to deal with the anxiety as a spiritual problem, but I still knew the decision was right.

A warning is in order. If you are not in fellowship with God, Satan can give you a false sense of peace. Therefore, never use peace or any one of these indicators alone as confirmation of God's will. They work together.

Decide and wait. Often it is wise to make your decision and then wait a day or two to let it settle before communicating it to others. If in a day or two you still know it is right, proceed with action. F. B. Meyer says,

Never act in panic nor allow men to dictate to thee; calm thyself and be still; force thyself into the quiet of thy closet until the pulse beats normally and the scare has ceased to disturb. When thou art most eager to act is the time when thou wilt make the pitiable mistakes. Do not say in thine heart what thou wilt or wilt not do, but wait upon God until He makes known His way. So long as that way is hidden, it is clear that there is not need of action, and that He accounts Himself responsible for all the results of keeping thee where thou art.[3]

Don't turn back. Whenever a right decision is made, Satan will send doubt and uncertainty. What God has shown you in the light, do not doubt in the dark. Beware of turning back when you have clearly found God's will. J. Oswald Sanders says, "Having put your hand to the plow, resolutely refuse to turn back. Otherwise, our Lord says you are 'not fit for the kingdom of God.' Never dig up in unbelief that which was sown in faith."[4]

Now act. Make all these steps in prayer and the Word; give God the chance to speak to you in all points; now act. Act in faith on what God has graciously shown you.

How to Pull Up Roots — Gently

Digging up a live plant and replanting it so that it lives is a delicate procedure. You begin loosening the plant by turning the shovel in the soil without touching the roots, carefully start to lift it out — ever so gently — keeping as much dirt on the roots and severing as few roots as possible. Then in replanting, you reverse the process giving the plant extra water, food, and care. We know how to move plants, but do we know how to move people? Especially little people — our children. Some roots will be severed, but it can be done without killing the spirit and crushing their happiness.

Here are some key points to consider as you move your family from one place to another. No move is ideal, but some are disasters. Seek a happy medium.

Prepare. The more you prepare for your move the less turmoil you will experience. Don't leave matters till the last minute. It will drain the entire family physically and emotionally.

Involve the family. Just as you would involve the family in the decision to move, now involve them in the process of moving. Get their opinions on what to move, how it will be done, and who will do it. Try to understand their feelings.

Timing. Whenever possible, move at a convenient time for the children. If they are in school, try to move during the summer. Also ascertain your wife's needs in the timing. You may need to consider going to the new location ahead of time by yourself.

Advance arrangements. Try to go to the new location well ahead of time to determine the situation. Where are the good schools? Where are the good churches? What is the housing market? Try to make arrangements for temporary lodging for the family before they arrive. Place more emphasis on the school and church situations than on proximity to your job or style of house. Whenever possible, move directly into your permanent housing.

Take time off. Take adequate time off on both ends of the move. In so doing you can give the move your full attention. Don't try to finish your work one day and move the next. If necessary, use accumulated vacation time to do this.

Get settled quickly. The sooner you are settled in your new house, the sooner it will be home to the family. Although you may get physically settled quickly, don't expect miracles in getting a family emotionally settled. It takes time to develop new relationships. After my family's last move, it took almost three years before one of my daughters finally announced, "I like this place better than our last one." Avoid reflecting verbally on the merits of the place you left: if you are content, it will greatly aid the children's adjustments. Find a church home quickly so the family can initiate Christian relationships: try to avoid months of church-hunting.

Above all, remember that home is not a house. You make the home. We have moved many times, and it has never brought serious readjustment problems for the children. There were strains and fears, but they were secure with us. God is your security; you are theirs.

How to Start a New Job

Your start on a new job is as important as your later performance. Some people get off to a bad start and never recover. First impressions last a long time. Early relationships, good and bad, color your enjoyment of work for years to come.

Knowing a few basic principles can avert great emotional trauma.

Concentrate. Plan to give your job 110 percent of your time and energy for the first month or two. That is the reason for getting totally settled first. Gain the family's support that this will be the priority. Learn your new job well.

Know what is expected. What is your job? Precisely what are you expected to do and know? Find out; assume nothing; make notes; do extra study. If you are unsure, ask questions. Ignorance is tolerated when you are new: it is inexcusable later.

Be a learner. Every job has its peculiarities — or at least the people do. Ask questions or directions. It is better to ask than to make a costly mistake. Do not feign ignorance, and don't act as if you know it all, but honestly try to learn.

Develop relationships. Get acquainted with your co-workers. They are generally more approachable when you are new. You can ask them questions and get help. Don't waste company time talking, but take every opportunity to communicate. This will lay the foundation for enjoyable working conditions and for a future witness.

Extra effort. Don't be afraid to put in extra hours and extra effort. Aim for quality performance. In a straight eight-hour factory or shop job, you may not be able to work additional time, but you can study on off hours. Most equipment has some kind of manual: use it. You will not be able to make this extra effort all the time, lest you cheat your family, but it is possible for the first few weeks or months of your job. It will provide good job "insurance."

Be a finisher. Unfinished work helps no one. You cannot sell a half-made product. Therefore develop a reputation for finishing what you start — on time. In earning a reputation for dependability and faithfulness, you reflect the character of God.

Discussion Questions

1. What are three key factors in finding God's will?
2. What would be valid reasons for *you* to make a job change? Have the group critique your reasons.
3. How can you discover your own motives in desiring a change?
4. How should you and the church react to one who is unemployed?
5. Discuss the key factors usually involved in losing a job.
6. How should a Christian react to losing a job?

CHAPTER 6

VOCATIONAL CHRISTIAN WORK

FULL-TIME Christian work was a career for which I had no interest or inclination. In my early Christian life I had no leading to it, nor was it attractive to me. Yet, about midnight one night in May 1972, I found myself on my knees telling God that I was available, and that I would resign from my career as an Air Force officer to be on the full-time staff of The Navigators.

Many were critical of my decision. Some were skeptical. One retired officer told me I was "insane." My grandmother cried. My wife was initially apprehensive. Most of my relatives were shocked. Others thought it was a great step of faith. The step seemed illogical, because I had only 6½ of my twenty years' service left until retirement. Many thought I should wait until then.

What led me to this decision?

I was not dissatisfied with my Air Force career. I was a major and had been given pleasing assignments. I had earned a Ph.D. and was in a good career field. In fact, I thoroughly enjoyed almost every aspect of my jobs, and the family enjoyed the life-style.

It was not that I was ineffective in ministry as a layman. In six years of teaching at the United States Air Force Academy I had been able to develop a significant outreach among the cadets. We saw several hundred young men receive Christ, and many of those became committed disciples who potentially will have a profound effect on the entire Air Force as they enter positions of leadership in the future.

It was not that the "offer" from The Navigators was too good to refuse. In fact, there was no "offer" at all. I would have to raise all my own support, since The Navigators operate as a faith mission with no guaranteed salary.

My real motivation stemmed from a deepening conviction from God concerning my spiritual gifts and my principle ministry for the future. As I became more involved in a discipling type of ministry as a layman, I found that I would have to limit my activities in either the job or my personal ministry to meet my family's needs adequately. As my children grew older and needed more of my time, my job was also becoming more demanding and time-consuming. Something had to give. At the same time, the results of our spiritual ministry to people clearly indicated gifts and abilities of that kind. I was leaning more and more strongly to people-centered interests rather than science-centered.

A significant factor was my longstanding relationship of almost seventeen years as a layman with The Navigators. I had experienced the results of this ministry in my own life and had reapplied it outward to others. I had already determined that if God did call me to a full-time outreach ministry, I would like to work with The Navigators.

Yet, in the process of making my decision there were no clear indicators. Counsel was divided. Pros and cons were fairly balanced. Certainly there would be no greater reward for vocational Christian work than for my work as a layman. Ultimately it came down to prayer and guidance from the Scriptures in making my final decision. And now, after three years of ministry, I have absolutely no regrets or second thoughts. God has clearly led and has given a settled peace.

Through this process — and in my task of counseling many

others considering a similar step — I have made several observations and drawn several conclusions about leaving the secular world to enter vocational Christian work. Note that the focus here is not on a student selecting vocational Christian work for his first occupation, though many of these ideas may be helpful in such a case.

Definition of Vocational Christian Work

Any discussion of vocational Christian work arouses certain feelings of fear, prejudice, or misconception. Even before attempting to define the terms, note that the expression "full-time Christian work" is not used. The premise of this book is that all secular work is spiritual and every Christian is "full-time." Therefore, the term *vocational* describes a person who has chosen some aspect of work in a church, Christian organization, or mission group as his occupation.

We will define vocational Christian work by two categories of function and two of location. The functions are —

Direct ministry function. This includes all ministry directed to people — either Christian or non-Christian. It includes pastors; Christian education directors; evangelists; missionaries in church planting; teachers in Christian schools; field staff of outreach organizations like Youth for Christ, Campus Crusade for Christ, and The Navigators; and Bible teaching or exposition. Broadly speaking, this function entails "speaking" gifts (teaching, exhortation, evangelism).

Serving or support function. This includes administrators, mechanics, secretaries, computer programmers, some executives, accountants, printers, builders, and myriad other roles necessary to any organization. This involves "serving" gifts (see 1 Peter 4:11).

The two categories of location are —

Foreign. This is any vocational Christian work conducted while living and ministering in another country and culture. It could include ministering to a distinct subculture in one's home country (such as the American Indian).

Home. This is ministry in the home country that involves no major travel or cultural adjustment.

The term *missionary* is generally applied to the "foreign"

category. I prefer a broader definition that includes persons ministering in a situation other than a local church in his own country (such as a missionary to students).

Myths of Vocational Christian Work

George Pennington dedicated himself to foreign missionary service in the closing meeting of a mission conference in his church. He was twenty-nine, married with two children, and a successful construction foreman. After three years of Bible school he was sent to a South American country to plant churches. Four years later George returned disillusioned, bitter, unsuccessful, and discouraged — a missionary "dropout." Why?

Let us probe George's history bit. He had never led another person to Christ. He was a mediocre Sunday school teacher. He earned straight C's in high school Spanish. Bible school was a struggle, but he was encouraged to press on with the explanation that his age made it more difficult. His mission board interviewed him primarily on doctrinal issues, rather than about functions he would be required to perform in his missionary work. When he arrived on the field, George found intense conflict among the senior missionaries and little positive training or supervision. Language study was disastrous. Then he found that although he could organize men to build a building, he could not bind people together around a spiritual objective. In construction work, he knew that if a man could not pound a nail straight after a month of trying, he never would and the best solution was to fire him. So George fired himself from the mission field and came home.

This illustration could just as well describe a pastor who failed to help a church progress, a youth director who was unable to work with people, or an evangelist who seldom led people to Christ. Missionary dropout rates are very high: 25–50 percent after the first term. There are multitudes of trained pastors who no longer lead churches.

It is no disgrace to leave vocational Christian work, any more than changing jobs or careers in any other context is a disgrace. Yet, in the eyes of the Christian community, that person is branded as a failure.

Misconceptions and myths about vocational Christian

work persist in the minds of many. Those considering it envision certain advantages and blessings. These are some of the myths:

Christian work is easy. Many people view Christian work as an escape from the secular rat race. However, most vocational Christian workers of my acquaintance put in from fifty to seventy hours a week. The schedule may be flexible, but it is never-ending. Rarely is there a real day off: the worker is always "on call." He is usually a motivated person, aware that he is living on "God's money," so he must produce well.

Seldom is Christian work easy. Even support people sense the call to work harder and longer. No church or organization will employ for long a staff person who shirks his work.

There is less pressure to produce. If anything, there is more pressure to demonstrate success in vocational Christian work. The problem is how to measure the product. But even with that ambiguity, people make evaluations. Some common measurements are number of meetings, attendance at meetings, conversions, baptisms, counseling sessions, and numerical growth in specific kinds of ministry. For support staff, the evaluation is like that in a secular job: work accomplished.

There is a more spiritual environment. This may hold true to a limited extent, but people in vocational Christian work are not automatically any more spiritual than those in secular work. They sin, they make mistakes, and they work in the flesh. At times their situation is more difficult, because in a secular environment there are no spiritual expectations; in Christian work the disappointment runs deep when matters are handled in an unspiritual way.

There is less conflict. Wherever people are involved, there is conflict. Sometimes the conflict escalates higher than in a secular context, because spiritual overtones give every issue a second face. Spiritual relationships in Christian work heighten the intensity of conflict. Churches split, pastors are dismissed, church staff cannot get along — all evidence that the threat of conflict is ever present.

But the Bible gives guidelines for resolving conflicts. When these guidelines are followed, a unified work environment is created — one that a secular context can never provide.

There is adequate time for prayer and Bible study. Virtually every person in vocational Christian work has more demands on his time than he can possibly fulfill. He battles to find sufficient time for prayer and Bible study.

Entering vocational Christian work requires a sacrifice. Many people suspect that the Christian worker will make great financial sacrifices. Is it a sacrifice to be in God's will? Certainly not: it is a privilege and blessing. Missionary Jim Elliot wrote before his martyrdom,

> He is no fool who gives what he cannot keep,
> To gain what he cannot lose.

Materially, God is the great provider and meets real needs. Riches rarely come to the Christian worker, but we must not assume that he is to be poverty-stricken as proof of his calling. Some may endure difficult times financially, but many positions in vocational Christian work now provide adequate salaries. The most difficult circumstance may be in "faith" missions that offer no guaranteed salary. More and more churches and organizations are beginning to raise wages scales on the biblical basis that "the laborer is worthy of his hire."

In many overseas mission assignments, there may be sacrifice in terms of health, family circumstances, and personal comfort. We would not minimize this sacrifice, but many missionaries never think in terms of sacrifice because they experience satisfaction in knowing they are where God wants them.

You must have a mysterious "call." Do you need some mysterious or emotional "call from God" to enter Christian work? Although some may claim this experience, it should not be the norm. We cannot support from the Scripture that such a call is different from a call to serve God in a secular vocation. In either case it requires finding God's will.

For Christian work, God simply begins to move a person in that direction by giving him fruit in a particular ministry and speaking to him through the Scriptures over a period of time. I would never discourage the missionary conference appeal, since God is not limited to one particular method of calling. But do not wait for that "feeling" or "call" before considering vocational Christian work. God may be trying to get your attention in other ways.

God may be speaking to you through the Word daily as you see more clearly the urgency of reaching the world for Christ. You may be seeing fruit in spiritual ministry now, indicating a gift that is greatly needed on the mission field. Since God is sovereign even in your acquaintances, He may be putting you in touch with people who will urge you to consider vocational Christian work. Allow God to lead quietly through your normal circumstances.

The need constitutes a call. Without question, the demand for men and women in Christian ministries greatly exceeds the supply. Nevertheless, a specific need does not constitute a call. Each person must consider his own special gifts and God's personal leading as well as the need. Desperate needs will always exist, but God does not necessarily call a person to fulfill what he observes as a need. God's "needs" *will* be met; man's "needs" will not and should not be met. Emotional appeals for help ring from every quarter, but they are not the call — just opportunities.

My gifts will be used more fully. The Scriptures do not teach that a spiritual gift should be used exclusively in a full-time ministry. There is no indication that they are more adequately or more fully utilized in that circumstance. Your gifts can be fully used in any context. However, each job in vocational work does require specialized types and capacities of gifts, so you may be excluded from certain ministries, or directed toward others, by your gifts and capacities.

The Great Need

The myths of the preceding section are meant, not to discourage, but only to inject realism. People *are* dying without Christ; mission efforts *are* being crippled by the lack of prepared personnel; countries *are* closing to missionaries; churches *are* desperate for qualified staff; mission boards *are* searching for people with special support qualifications. Matthew 9:37,38 will always be true: "Then He said to His disciples, 'The harvest is plentiful, but the workers are few. Therefore beseech the Lord of the harvest to send out workers into His harvest.' "

But the true need can be fulfilled only by *committed, qualified,* and *trained* people. There is no room for incompetence. God's business should be done with excellence. Standards must be high, and the training thorough.

Every Christian should consider the possibility of vocational Christian work. Give God the opportunity to lead. Inquire about opportunities. You may be gifted, but are you available? You may be available, but are you trained? And, above all, are you committed to Christ and maturing spiritually?

Paradoxically, I must admit that God has used some very unlikely people in the past — people who, in man's eyes, were not qualified or trained. But they had the lost of the world on their hearts, and they were called by God, as evidenced by the fruit of their lives. Who would have selected Peter (a fisherman) or William Carey (a shoemaker) or D. L. Moody (a salesman)? Though we as humans plan, evaluate, organize, and decide, God supercedes such limitations. The man or woman does not exist whom God cannot use.

Guidelines for Considering Vocational Christian Work

Most Christians, at some time in their lives, sense an urging or an interest to consider vocational Christian work. After receiving a specific call from God, you must answer this important question: "If I enter a Christian ministry, how can I be certain I will be effective?" Here are some suggested guidelines to help you determine if you should make a move to Christian work.

Scriptural qualifications. The most important guideline is to meet the biblical qualifications for church officers in 1 Timothy 3 and Titus 1. They deal with an individual's spiritual maturity, reputation, family life, and personal walk with God. Though every Christian should seek to meet these standards, they constitute a necessary minimum for anyone considering vocational Christian work or positions of spiritual authority. If this standard is violated, the ministry will be corrupted. Therefore, examine yourself in the light of these requirements.

Discerning your spiritual gifts and abilities. God has endowed every person with particular gifts and abilities. You should be able to evaluate your abilities. If you do not have a reasonable estimate of your own abilities (Rom. 12:3), how can you determine where to make your contribution? How can you know? Only by the fruit of your life.

Look at results, not potential. If you are an evangelist, where are your converts? If you are a teacher, have you had successful teaching experiences? If you are a leader, where are your followers? Your gifts and abilities should match the task to which you are called. A good heart and a willing spirit are not substitutes for God-controlled ability. The former attempts, and the latter accomplishes.

Determining the Extent and Capacity of Spiritual Gifts

You need to see the results of your gifts and abilities. But even beyond that, you need to have an idea of the extent of your abilities — in other words, your capacity. Not everyone who has a particular gift can produce the same results; there will be differences in effectiveness. You may be able to lead a small group of people, but not a church of four hundred. You may communicate well to large groups, but cannot teach or train leadership individually. You may have led several personal acquaintances to Christ, but cannot evangelize strangers.

Determine not only *what* you can do, but also *how well* you do it. Training will certainly increase your effectiveness, but it will not greatly increase your capacity. A mature person should have a knowledge of his capacity as well as his gifts.

But if you *do* have the right abilities and gifts, you bear a responsibility to God to be available to Him full-time. Don't hide behind false modesty or a weak estimate of yourself. William Carey considered himself to be slow in mind, yet he influenced India for Christ by translating the Scriptures into a monumental number of Indian languages. Determination and diligence will succeed where fleshly ability fails. But think of the impact on the world of demonstrated ability *with* determination and diligence!

Get evaluation. Always secure objective evaluation from others of what you have done and can do. Be specific. Cut through the niceties of polite compliments. Your life is at stake, and no amount of kind words can replace truth. You should raise questions such as —

- What are a few of my strengths?

- How do you know? Specifically, how have you seen this demonstrated?

- What are a few of my weaknesses?

- If I were to enter Christian ministry, what would I do well?

- What would I have a difficult time doing?

- How do you feel I would do at (name the task you are considering)?

- What evidence have you actually seen that gives you that feeling?

Ask several people who know you to help in this way. You may even ask non-Christians, such as your employer: not for counsel, but for evaluation. At this point you are gathering information and evaluation, not asking counsel. Concentrate on facts, and write down the key points of each evaluation, then begin correlating them to see if some agreement emerges.

Do not neglect to evaluate yourself. Even with your emotional involvement, you can be factual and honest about yourself to some extent. And, of course, your mate should evaluate you as objectively as possible.

Family unity. If you are married, you must make this decision as a couple, especially if it significantly affects your income or geographical location. Even the children should be part of the decision-making if they are old enough to understand the implications of such a move. In Christian work, it is important that the family be fully united in the decision and in the work.

The Challenge

There is great need and opportunity. If you are qualified and called, vocational Christian work will give you fulfillment far beyond your expectations. But it cannot be used as an escape: you will be the same person with the same spiritual problems. You will encounter the same conflicts and power struggles. As Christians we are in a battle for the lives of men and women, so opposition from Satan is inevitable wherever we are.

A successful accountant recently asked me about accounting in a Christian organization. He liked his work and was having a ministry with people. But he wanted to see his efforts contribute to an enterprise of lasting value, rather than counting money for people trying to get rich. He subsequently joined the staff of a Christian organization in which he could use his accounting skills.

I have no regrets for my personal decision to enter vocational Christian service. God clearly led, and I am greatly fulfilled. But I do value those thirteen years in a secular job. They were excellent preparation.

When all the facts are in and you know what God wants, you must act. No ledger sheet of pros and cons will act for you. You must step out on *raw* faith. That is real life, in a secular job or in vocational Christian work: living totally by faith. There is no substitute. It alone brings fulfillment.

> And the LORD said to Moses, "Is the LORD's power limited? Now you shall see whether my word will come true for you or not" (Num. 11:23).

Discussion Questions

1. Define vocational Christian work.
2. What are reasons for entering vocational Christian work?
3. Discuss the differences of ministry in a secular job and in vocational Christian work.
4. Discuss the differences and relationships between calling, gifts, and needs.
5. Discuss the statement, "Every Christian should consider vocational Christian work."
6. If a person is qualified and called, what is the best age to enter vocational Christian work?
7. What are advantages and disadvantages of being in a secular job for a period of time before entering vocational Christian work?
8. Is there a gap between "laymen" and "clergy"? Explain your answer. If your answer is yes, discuss what can be done to bridge the gap.

PART II

CIRCUMSTANCES

Each of the following chapters applies to a particular type of job. Therefore you need only to read the ones applicable to your circumstance. For example, if you are salaried and travel a great deal, read chapters 8 and 14. If you are paid hourly and have unusual working hours, read chapters 7 and 14. If you are a woman with a salaried job, read chapters 8 and 10.

Do not read these chapters without first reading part I. Chapters 7 to 14 are incomplete by themselves, but serve as extensions of the material in part I.

CHAPTER 7

THE HOURLY EMPLOYEE

JOHN CLARKSON was bored. Just plain bored. In fact, he was both bored and pressured. For fifteen years he had been going to work day after day, week after week, and dreading every minute of it. He worked on an automobile assembly line and had performed essentially the same tasks all this time. There were variations — new model, different technique, and occasionally a different function on the line. But after a few days each variation became monotonous. Finally he admitted to himself, "I hate work."

John began finding excuses to miss work, actually became sick more frequently, and was a terror to live with at home. His wages were substantial, and so were the benefits. He started "living for the weekend" and poured his life and money into hobbies and projects. But eventually he finished remodeling his house, and he lost interest in the hobbies.

He felt worse, because he was a Christian. He recognized his continuing discontent and knew he should not feel the way he did. So a guilt complex set in. He was torn between his real feelings and his Christian responsibility to be "on top" and happy. Even church and Christian involvement became a burden, and he started to withdraw.

Then two significant and unexpected events occurred. One evening the phone rang, and a weeping woman asked if John would help her. It was Alice — Harry Jackson's wife. Harry, who worked next to John at the factory, had just suffered a heart attack and was in critical condition in the hospital. Alice said she knew John was "religious" and wondered if he and his wife could talk to her husband. John was surprised: he and Alice had met only once, at a company picnic. On another occasion, feeling guilty about not witnessing, John had given Harry a tract.

The second incident involved Raymond Erickson, a senior executive in the automobile company John worked for. John and Raymond were members of the same church, but they had had only minor contact via Sunday school classes. Raymond was wealthy, successful, and very busy. John was envious of him — his wealth, his standing in the church as "the Christian businessman," and his status in industry. Now gossip had it that Raymond's wife had left him and they were facing divorce! The gossip proved true.

The divorce incident shattered John's illusion of the ideal job. The heart attack incident resulted in Harry and Alice's both receiving Christ. This marked the beginning of a new view of life and work for John. He had a purpose: to reach his co-workers and neighbors for Christ. His job was the same — but he was a changed man. He saw why God had put him in the factory and became reconciled to the circumstance. He deeply appreciated his regular schedule and his ability to spend time with his family.

Each of us can relate to John Clarkson, especially if our job is similar to his. He found an answer. How can you find one? That is what this chapter is about — finding an answer in your particular circumstance.

This chapter speaks to the hourly employee — the man or woman who is paid by the hour and works a regular, eight-hour day. The job may vary from factory worker or truckdriver to salesclerk or office employee. Some are very enjoyable, some very difficult, and some easy. But they all have the similar elements of regular hours and pay according to the time spent on the job. The pay varies from low to very good. But even if you find the work satisfying and have financial security, you still face the question of how the job fits into the whole of your life.

Advantages and Benefits

In many ways this kind of job is the most liberating and advantageous of all. As in most jobs there are two dimensions: the spiritual and the physical. By *spiritual*, I mean your heart attitude and the perspective of why God has placed you there. By *physical*, I mean the actual circumstance of your work and schedule. Your goal is to develop the spiritual and take advantage of the physical.

Regularity of schedule. Though you may consider the regularity of your job a boredom factor, in reality it gives you the freedom and ability to plan your time. You can depend on certain nights being open. Your weekends can be planned well in advance. Rarely will work interfere with your plans. You may still experience a time crunch, but it will not be as a result of your job. Take advantage of that job regularity to control your off-the-job time, so as to be with your family, develop spiritually, and have a personal ministry.

A defined job. Most jobs of this nature are clearly defined. You know exactly what to do and know how it is to be done. You know when you have finished, and when you leave the site, you can forget about the job until the next day. You may lack personal supervision, but usually there is little question of what is expected of you. Many people do not want the pressure or the worries of supervising or sales. In clearly defined work, there is great freedom of mind.

Stability of location. Persons employed in hourly jobs move less frequently than others. A forced move within a particular company is unlikely unless there is major economic problem or a plant closes. With seniority comes additional stability. If you have a highly marketable skill, you may choose to move, but rarely will it be required. This stability allows you to establish deep roots and friendships in one community. It provides a great opportunity for long-term witness and family maturity.

Sense of definite accomplishment. Most jobs in this category have a recognizable product. When you finish a day's work you can see what you have accomplished. In jobs requiring physical stamina, you know you have worked hard. There is a peaceful rest to one who labors in this way; there can be great satisfaction in seeing the work of your hands. If your personality is such that you like to see a task finished, you are in the right place.

Increasing security in a job. In most jobs of this kind, you achieve additional security with time because of seniority, union membership, or experience. With the exception of seasonal or contract work, you find that if you are dependable and competent, you will gain increasing security. This can be a significant advantage in freeing your mind and emotions to concentrate on other things. It must never be a crutch or cop-out for change, but in the right perspective this security can greatly enhance your ministry.

Disadvantages and Restraints

With any job there are disadvantages and restraints. They are not insurmountable or unchangeable, but recognizing them will help you to deal with them and give insight to your personal circumstances.

Immobility. When you have established yourself in an hourly job, it is often difficult to relocate unless you have a highly marketable skill. Therefore you tend to stay in the same location and same job. Moving brings risks. Where the skilled labor supply is abundant, finding a different job may be out of the question. You lose seniority in starting over in a new company.

Pay. Though the wage scales in many laboring and skilled jobs have risen markedly in recent years, they usually do not rise far above the level of necessity. Wage limits exist and are directly related to the hours worked. Many hourly jobs remain near the minimum wage, especially for women workers.

Boredom. As illustrated at the beginning of this chapter, boredom is a reality in jobs involving a repetitive task. If you enjoy change and variety, monotony in a job is a significant drawback. Few hourly jobs offer much variety, though work that brings frequent contact with the public may be less monotonous.

Pressure to produce. In hourly jobs you are hired for what you produce. If you do not produce, you will lose the job. You must make so many parts, cut so many pieces of metal, type so many letters, repair a certain portion of a car, or accomplish some reasonable task at a specific rate of speed.

These conditions create pressure. You may not be able to work at your own pace even if you do superior work. The pressure to produce can affect you emotionally and even spiritually. If this is your problem, how can you deal with it?

1. Determine whether you are capable of producing as much as the management demands. In most cases you can.

2. If you cannot keep up, try to move to another position in the company where you can do what is required.

3. Don't fight the pressure with a bad attitude, but really try to do what is expected. You will find your capacity increasing if you are emotionally calm.

Spiritual Dangers

Every job entails spiritual dangers. Most do not result directly from the job, but from an attitude or response to circumstances. Each job has certain characteristics that tend to invite the spiritual problems. Knowing these will help you to recognize and deal with them. Most of the solutions to these problems have been dealt with in earlier chapters.

Bitterness. When you have little choice in the specific requirements of your job, bitterness can easily creep in — bitterness toward your boss, the company, its organization, working conditions, and your co-workers. It can develop if you question why God didn't create you with more intelligence, why you did not get more education, or why you do not have a skill that would allow you to be in a better job.

For the Christian, bitterness is ultimately directed toward God Himself, for it obscures the fact that God has placed you in those circumstances. Worst of all, bitterness never helps — it always hurts you and others. "See to it that no one comes short of the grace of God; that no root of bitterness springing up causes trouble, and by it many be defiled" (Heb. 12:15).

Lack of self-esteem. In our society, little honor is given to people in hourly jobs. This is an error, since many "professional" people do not provide the daily necessities of our lives. They do provide research and planning, but the "working people" are the ones who put the plans into practice, who really do the job. You can be deluded into comparing your work with that of salaried or professional people and in so doing develop a low estimate of yourself. In God's sight, all are equal. No one will be judged on his type of employment, but rather on how he lived in that job. God made you, and He put you where you are. Do not fight against God, but give Him the opportunity to use you where you are now.

Desire for more money. Money tempts almost everyone. There never seems to be enough: "enough" is always a little more than you have now. In low-paying jobs, finances can be a constant struggle. Instead of lowering their standard of living, men tend to scrimp and save, work overtime, work at a second job, and put their wives to work. People want to buy a better house, get a newer car, get better furniture, eat out more often, buy recreational equipment, and take elaborate vacations. When the desire for more money becomes a driving force, giving to the Lord's work decreases, the family is neglected, and spiritual warmth fades and threatens to disappear. You need to feed, house, and clothe your family, but you need not do it with plastic credit cards, time payments, or loans. Live within your means.

My parents set a strong example for me. They had little, but they used what they had wisely. They never spent more than they had. Charging anything was rare. Each paycheck was apportioned to meet specific needs, and when it ran out, the buying stopped.

Lack of ambition. In jobs of a repetitive nature, or where our qualifications limit us, it is easy to lose motivation and ambition. It is common to dream or hope for something different or better; but false hopes lead to poor performance or even to being fired. Our employer should prosper by our presence and work: does he? We should exercise godly ambition and see what God opens up for us. We must keep a good testimony by working well and maintaining a good attitude.

Social pressure. Rough talk, unkind remarks, dirty jokes, and pressure to conform seem ever present in many hourly jobs. The temptation to conform is often overwhelming. This, then, leads the Christian to a double life — one mode of conduct at work, another mode elsewhere.

We will either influence or be influenced by every group we join. We must avoid being a "holier-than-thou" person who cannot relate well to other people. We should be with them and be their friend. But we need not conform to their actions or motivations. We should not use the "I-don't-do-that-because-I'm-a-Christian" approach. Rather, if we live by our convictions quietly, God will give us many opportunities to witness. "And do not be conformed to this world, but be transformed by the renewing of your mind, that you may prove what the will of God is, that which is good and acceptable and perfect" (Rom. 12:2).

In the Old Testament, Daniel is an excellent example of a man who refused to conform and whom God subsequently blessed. Whenever you are tempted to conform, ask these questions:

1. Is there any command in Scripture about this?

2. What would be gained by conforming?

3. Would I do this in the presence of my family or other Christians?

4. Will this add to or detract from my testimony for Christ?

Ethical problems at work. In most jobs some ethical problems will arise. A few of these are work slowdowns, falsifying documents, substandard workmanship, misuse of company time or funds, covering up for other employee's wrongdoing, and lying in various forms. Every situation has its own complexities and extenuating circumstances. However, you must apply scriptural guidelines to each case.

I would not attempt to give counsel to any specific job situation, but these are general guidelines:

1. Is this directly contrary to Scripture? If so, you must obey God. (Acts 4:19,20: "But Peter and John answered and said to them, 'Whether it is right in the sight of God to give heed to you rather than to God, you be the judge; for we cannot

stop speaking what we have seen and heard.' ")

2. When in doubt, seek godly counsel, both from a Christian in your kind of job and another mature Christian.

3. Pray, search the Scriptures, and confirm your convictions.

4. Stick with your convictions, even if it means losing your job.

Separating your work and life. When a job is distasteful and unfulfilling, we tend to segregate it from the rest of life. It becomes like a bad habit or a chronic pain — we just try to ignore it. We live for the evening or the weekend. If you pass forty hours each week with that attitude, you waste 25 percent of your total life and 40 percent of your waking hours. What a tragedy to spend that much of your time in a depressing, disagreeable activity! It must contribute to your self-esteem, your ministry to others, and your total life. Remember that God gave you that job to reach people — not just to put bread on the table. Integrate your job into your life and stop living in two worlds.

Guidelines and Suggestions

No two jobs are alike, but many have similarities. For the employee who is paid an hourly wage, basic problems and characteristics have been identified. Now you need to know how to take advantage of your particular set of life circumstances. Here are some ideas to help you get started.

Take advantage of your schedule. Since you have a regular schedule, you should put it to good advantage. You can plan a week in advance, or even a month. Refer to chapter 3 for suggestions on priorities and use of time. You need not allow activities to eat up your time; schedule activities that suit your objectives and priorities. For example, you could schedule —

— at least two family nights each month;

— attendance at your children's key activities (e.g., concerts, sports events); be selective;

— at least one social contact per month with a non-Christian couple;

— church activities of your choosing;

— personal Bible study.

Use your Saturday for maximum accomplishment. For most people Saturday is a wasted day. We rise later, putter around the house, read the paper, have an extra cup of coffee, run a few errands, watch part of a ball game, and soon it's gone — with little accomplished. The one day over which you have complete control — wasted. We should plan our Saturdays well and not let them just slip away. These guidelines may prove helpful:

1. Get up at a reasonably early hour and have a *good* devotional time. It is the one unhurried time you can count on in the week.

2. Use the morning for study, Sunday school lesson preparation, or preparation for next week's activities.

3. If you have a large project (e.g., painting or building), plan ahead, get the materials beforehand, and work hard at it. It is often best to do this in the afternoon, but on hot days start earlier.

4. Avoid little projects and errands. Use the time just before the evening meal on workdays to do these.

5. Give your wife a couple of hours to herself. You take care of the children (and not just while she does the shopping).

6. Avoid the big time trap of a four-hour game on TV. This is not always wrong, but note that it is about 15 percent of your free time. Don't waste it (though some large projects indoors permit having a radio or TV set nearby).

7. Plan your Saturday nights a month ahead. Make one of them an evening out with your mate. Use another to have a couple in. Another should include a family activity. Spend at least one of them at home. (Again, don't make TV the center of your home life; limit its use for *all* the family.)

Live within your finances. One of the greatest pressures on a marriage comes from spending beyond a family's income. Learn to live within your means. It may require drastically cutting back on spending. Return or sell those "things" that have put a financial millstone around your neck; learn to eat more simply; above all, give generously and gladly to the Lord's work.

Develop neighborhood relationships. God has placed you

in a specific neighborhood for a purpose. Most of your neighbors probably hold jobs similar to yours and can relate to your circumstances. Get to know them. Open up your home and seek to be an influence and a witness.

Develop an attitude of excellence toward your job. Whatever your job, do it the best you can. This was discussed earlier, but it bears repeating. Much of your witness is effected by how you work — or don't work.

Pray for your co-workers. Remember that God placed you in your job to influence others to Christ. You need to pray regularly for your co-workers, asking God to convict them and to allow you opportunities to witness verbally to them.

CHAPTER 8

THE SALARIED EMPLOYEE

CHUCK HORNER felt trapped. For three years he had worked as a machinist in a farm implement manufacturing company. He was good at his job, and it paid moderately well. But as he looked around, he saw men nearing retirement age who had done the same job for nearly thirty years. He dreaded a future like that. So, on meager savings, the GI bill, and part-time work by both Chuck and his wife, he struggled through college and earned an engineering degree.

Chuck anticipated a new freedom, both in the nature of his work and in his finances. He felt liberated. He accepted a job with a large company at a very good salary. The first year was like a honeymoon — good pay, regular hours, and good working conditions. He really liked being on a salary and not punching a time clock. Then some unexpected things began to happen.

The company landed a large contract. New people were hired, but they were untrained and unqualified. The contract called for strict deadlines, and production became a pressurized situation. Chuck had major responsibility for fulfilling the contract. He appreciated the challenge, but his eight-hour days stretched to ten and twelve hours. Soon the work encompassed Saturday mornings. Pressure increased to the point where he experienced tension both at work and at home.

Chuck began to wonder where all his freedom went. Because he was salaried, he now had more work and more responsibility for the same pay. He discovered a new set of problems: in the pressured work environment, he made a critical error in his calculations and was held personally responsible by his boss.

Suddenly Chuck's job and his future were in jeopardy. The next ten days were a nightmare — twelve-to-fourteen hours of work each day with incredible pressure. Now the salaried position didn't seem quite so attractive. Reality had crashed in on him, and he was working very hard for that extra money.

Chuck's case may not be like yours, but it is like many responsible salaried positions. In this chapter I deal with the kind of job that pays a stipulated salary for a month's work and requires doing whatever is necessary to fulfill a stated objective. There are basically two kinds of salaried jobs: *product oriented* and *people oriented* (middle management).

Product-oriented roles include engineering, scientific research, teaching, accounting, computer programming, editing, and some skilled crafts. They are jobs that make you responsible for producing a definite product or result; they do not require managing others to produce.

Middle-management positions include foremen, plant supervisors, lead engineers, sales managers, and supermarket and department store managers. Generally these workers are a step removed from the actual product or service.

Advantages and Benefits

Much of the previous chapter applies to both salaried and hourly workers. There are, however, some differences, in the job and in the kinds of persons who would be employed in such jobs.

Job satisfaction. In most cases, a person takes a salaried job more from choice than from necessity. Therefore salaried workers are more likely to enjoy their work and experience job satisfaction. They may be the kind of person who likes a certain measure of responsibility and dislikes punching a time clock. Most likely, they were aware of the specifics of the job beforehand and therefore could anticipate job satisfaction.

Pay. In salaried jobs the pay is usually higher, which gives more economic freedom. But people tend to buy nicer houses, better furniture, and better food, so often the pay ironically seems to go no further and budgets remain tight. The danger exists of not giving any more to the Lord's work than people with less income.

Status. In man's eyes, this kind of job does carry status. You are viewed as a "professional" person. In God's economy there is no difference, but the world's system makes these distinctions. Instead of becoming proud, take advantage of it: let it be the platform from which you speak, witness, and minister. You will have a natural "in" to others in similar professions. Thus you should use your platform for God's glory.

Mobility. A salaried person has mobility. Frequently he is in a field that is not dependent on the seniority system or limited by function to one company, so he is free to move to another company or to change positions within a company. He is not locked into one job or geographical area. Mobility results in increased availability to God for ministry opportunities.

Motivation. A salaried job will often be highly motivating and challenging. It tends to be less routine or monotonous. There is generally some measure of responsibility for people or projects, and that opportunity motivates many. This is an excellent kind of job for one who enjoys freedom, responsibility, and creativity.

Disadvantages and Restrictions

With more pay comes more responsibility. With responsibility come restrictions. So along with the advantages, you do inherit some disadvantages that must be weighed and balanced with your personality, gifts, and abilities.

Schedule. When you are salaried, you must be more available and responsive to your employer's needs. Your schedule may be more crowded, and there will be times when you must give extra time and effort to the job. You are less in control of your schedule. If you accept a salaried position, you inherit with it a more complex responsibility and schedule.

Pressure. In an hourly job there is a pressure to produce at a certain rate. In a salaried job the pressure is greater and the means of accomplishing a task less clearly defined. The work depends more on ability than on manual labor in a given time. Evaluation of your production is usually on a subjective or qualitative basis rather than on objective facts or finite measure. It may not depend on what you have done, but on what people who work for you have done. It may be difficult to leave the pressure behind at the job, and you have to live with it during nonworking time.

Ambition. As a salaried employee you are paid according to your position and job description. Therefore advancement presents itself as a goal, and ambition becomes a factor in your thinking. This is not wrong, but it must be handled in a spiritual manner. Chapter 4 provides specific help for this problem.

Responsibility. With increased salary come increased responsibilities. You cross the line from wages for work produced to wages for responsibilities carried. This is not a disadvantage but may bring restrictions, since it exacts a toll in time and emotional resources. Some people respond well to responsibility: if so, that makes it an advantage, not a restriction. If you don't like responsibility with accountability, you are not well-suited to this kind of job.

Spiritual Dangers

The spiritual dangers of a salaried job are not unique. Yet a few stand out as worthy of mention.

- Pride;
- Materialism;
- Ambition.

Pride can enter in many ways: pay, position, social status, education, and ability. Pride always has destructive results. It causes conflicts, strains relationships, and stunts spiritual growth and outreach. Whenever pride begins to emerge in your life, deal with it immediately before it becomes so ingrained that you no longer recognize it. No one is immune to pride.

Materialism encroaches on your life even when you don't seem to have money to buy material things. But materialism is an attitude — an improper desire for things. And the more "things" you have, the more you want. Seldom is the desire related to necessities, but rather to luxuries. Guard against materialism as a prime motivator in your life.

Ambition has been mentioned as a disadvantage. It is also a significant spiritual danger. Keep your motives aligned with God's will and your own abilities.

Guidelines and Suggestions

Your response to your job and schedule determines your control over it, or its control over you. Here are some practical suggestions to help you function more profitably in a salaried job.

Determine your capacity. Since promotion and responsibility are natural outgrowths of a salaried position, it is imperative that you know your limitations as well as your strengths. You may be promoted, but what will it cost you in terms of your family and ministry? Do not allow yourself to be promoted beyond your capacity or you, your family, and ministry will all suffer. Life is too short to force yourself beyond the limits God has sovereignly built into your life. Chapter 4 gives more help in this matter.

Use Saturdays well. Saturday is the largest single block of time over which you have control. Most people waste it. Refer to the detailed discussion in chapter 7.

Avoid excessive overtime. As a salaried worker you are obligated to respond to the demands of additional work. However, overtime should not become a habit, since it greatly affects your family life and ministry. If extra work becomes a pattern, evaluate these factors:

1. Do I have extra work because I am not getting my regular work done? Can I concentrate and accomplish more in the regular time?

2. Am I working overtime just for the impression it makes on people?

3. Have I simply gotten into a habit of working extra hours?

4. Is the extra work unnecessary?

If your answer to any of these questions is yes, you are the basic cause of the overtime and should make some immediate adjustments. If the overtime is necessary on an extended basis, try these steps:

1. Keep a record of what you do for two or three weeks.

2. Take that record and discuss the situation with your supervisor to try to reduce the overtime. Make suggestions that will help him solve the problems instead of throwing all the burden of a solution on him.

3. If there is no other way, decide if you really want to continue in that job, since this may be God's way of directing you toward other employment.

In this process do *not* try to avoid all overtime. Extra hours are a legitimate part of your responsibility as a salaried employee. You simply want to avoid excessive, continuing overtime.

Schedule family time. Your family is always more important than your job, so give time with them high priority. In the midst of pressure, overtime, and trying to advance in your job, it is all too easy to neglect those most important to you. When you plan your week or month, schedule specific time with your family. Make your vacations special times with them — doing things that fit their idea of family fun.

Use your finances well. As your salary increases, you will tend to spend more and live more extravagantly. God has a purpose in giving you that extra money: it means you should probably give more to your church and missions. Pray about those expenditures that contribute only to comfort and status and do not fulfill a vital need.

As Christians we are responsible to God for *all* our money, not just the part we give to His work. We should invest in people, not things. It is good to avoid getting into debt on depreciating items (furniture, cars, clothes) and to wait until we have saved enough to pay cash for them.

Use your position well. Frequently a salaried job carries some status in the company or community. Use that status for God's glory, not your own. You can reach people whom no one else can. I have frequently found that I can get a hearing for the gospel because I am an engineer or because I was in the Air Force. Other engineers or Air Force people listen because they have confidence that I can realistically relate to their circumstances and situations. To the world, you are more identified with what you do than with who you are.

Avoid pushing your position or status to a point of pride. A simple question to ask as a safeguard in this matter is, "Why do I want people to know my status — to admire me, or to win a hearing for the gospel?" Your motives are the key.

CHAPTER 9

THE HOMEMAKER

WHEN BEVERLY graduated from business college at age twenty-one she obtained a well-paying, stimulating position in a growing company. She worked for two years, then married an engineer she met in the career group at her church. In the first two years of their marriage, two baby boys were born. The adjustments Beverly needed to make were tremendous. She no longer controlled her own time, finances were tight, she felt pressured by the unending needs of her husband and two sons. She wanted to have a spiritual influence in her neighborhood and church, but could never seem to find the time. She began to resent the demands on her in her home and felt chronically fatigued, often sick.

Homemakers like Beverly number in the thousands — perhaps millions: vaguely dissatisfied, unchallenged, harried, tired. What a distressing waste of potential, energy, and capability!

Many women have been influenced by the recent vehement attacks on the career of homemaking. The inferences are made that the value of work is based on the salary level and therefore, since homemakers receive no salary, the work must have little worth.

Every woman who feels called by God to remain in her home needs to have —

— biblical conviction for the value of her work;

— an efficient plan for maximizing her own potential as a person and as a worker.

Proverbs 31 describes a wife and mother who has the approval of God. She is efficient, industrious, organized, energetic, generous, family oriented, dignified, kind, and spiritually mature. The job of homemaker is not identical with housekeeper, though that is part of the work; perhaps more than any other employment, it is a reflection of the character and personality of a woman. Homemaking is one of the few jobs in which completed results can be observed, both in terms of a house that demonstrates the care and creative capacity of the woman, and people (husband and perhaps children) who reflect the daily interaction with the wife and mother. Later in the chapter we suggest specific ways to express these traits positively in the home.

Advantages and Benefits

Independence. A homemaker has considerable freedom to establish and follow her own work patterns. She does not report to an "employer," though there are responsibilities to other members of the family. She can set her own work guidelines and standards. She can determine her own priorities and interests and adjust much of her time accordingly.

Shirley and Joanne were friends who typified differing styles of homemaking. They were in their late twenties; each had two preschool children; their husbands worked eight-to-five shifts; they attended the same church; and they lived on the same block in homes of similar design.

But there the resemblance stopped. Shirley was an energetic "people" person. Her working day began at 6 A.M. when she whirled through routine housework for an hour. After breakfast with the family, she would play with her children. Then she would head for a Bible study, to a friend's house, a craft class, a church activity. Or, if she were home, her house would resound with activity — people coming and going, the phone jangling. No one ever defined Shirley's home as immaculate or serene, but everyone was happy to be there.

Joanne began her day by a careful check of a detailed schedule prepared the previous week. Menus were precisely outlined, work was organized, social engagements were planned well in advance. Her children were always clean and always well-dressed, with organized activities and creative projects. She maintained a few close and loyal friendships.

Two different women, each with the freedom to express herself in and through her home.

Creativity. A flexible schedule allows for time to include creative projects. Some are naturally a part of homemaking. Others, while they contribute, are more a personal expression of ability and taste. A few of these creative interests are —

— decorating;
— crafts (a wide choice);
— clothes design;
— creative writing;
— study of nutrition;
— gardening (indoors and out);
— music.

And these activities can expand, change, and grow as a woman's interests change.

I recently became involved in just such a project. Because of the small size of our present living room, we were forced to dispense with a cabinet that housed my husband's stereo components. They sit now on bare shelves in one corner of the room. With my husband's skeptical approval, I am "growing" a stereo cabinet. Green plants are appearing around, above, and under the shelves. The arrangement may prove temporary — for now, it's a challenge!

In a real sense, a home is an extension of a woman's personality, where she is free to demonstrate her interests and talents to the fullest extent time will allow.

Schedule flexibility. Few jobs allow the flexibility of homemaking. Although it is essential to efficient housekeeping to follow some kind of schedule, that can be arranged according to the requirements of the family and the personal needs and interests of each woman. Often a woman can reduce or increase her work load to suit her standards and activities. Scheduling and use of time will be discussed in more detail at the end of the chapter.

Ministry opportunities. A home is an ideal place to demonstrate the love of Christ. Because she has a relatively free schedule, a homemaker can invite others into her home — individuals or groups — for specific spiritual purposes. A home can be used for Bible studies, evangelistic meetings, dinners with a non-Christian couple, and time with a needy Christian or non-Christian friend. Some mothers of young children might feel they cannot use their homes for such activities. That is not valid. If you cannot conveniently host a dinner, put your children to bed and invite someone for a late dessert and coffee afterward. Find a reliable baby-sitter to care for children during a Bible study, and share the expense with the group. Allow God to use you and your home.

Support of husband in family goals. An enriching and satisfying aspect of homemaking is the involvement with a husband and children. Every other job focuses on production, people, or profit unrelated to your personal life. In your home you have the privilege of giving your life and energy to something that is part of you — your husband and your children. To be involved in their goals is one of God's highest callings. Although the husband is ultimately responsible for making decisions in a family, the wife sets the atmosphere in the home where those decisions are carried out. Usually she has the major day-to-day influence on the children.

Without this perspective of family support, housework and the other functions of homemaking become empty and purposeless. The objective is not a clean house, but an atmosphere for family growth. The specific activities of a homemaker, though somewhat satisfying in themselves, are fulfilling as they contribute to building and supporting the family. The biblical principle of giving and then receiving even more in return is nowhere more evident than in a wife's giving to her husband and children.

Disadvantages and Restraints

Monotony. Many tasks in the home are routine. Boredom can quickly result if precautions are not taken. The work must be done, but monotony can be reduced by creative planning. Whenever possible, do the routine, least enjoyable chores first in your schedule. If the work does not require mental concentration, use the time to listen to profitable radio programs or tape recordings, to tell Bible stories to your children, and even to talk on the telephone. One of the best investments in our home is a long cord on the telephone receiver so that I can move about as I talk. Keep in mind that monotony is not unique to housekeeping but is a standard aspect of many jobs. The homemaker is fortunate in that she has more flexibility of schedule and more opportunity to inject interest into her job than most other workers.

Confinement. There is an element of what pioneer women used to call "cabin fever" that seems to strike most homebound women now and then. It is the lack of freedom to be out of the home and around other adults consistently. Mothers of small children find this especially true. They develop a conscientious responsibility for their children but feel tied down and isolated.

If a sense of confinement becomes a problem, you can alleviate it. Invite other women in similar circumstances into your home. Arrange for responsible care for your children while you do something that is personally stimulating for you. Express your frustration to your husband: he just may have helpful ideas. In fact, he may even arrange free time for you by taking care of the children.

Long hours. No other occupation requires an employee to be on call twenty-four hours a day, seven days a week, year after year. For women who do not know how to schedule their work, and who fail to make time for spiritual development and personal interests, the long hours can be devastating. Every homemaker needs to evaluate her work load periodically to eliminate unnecessary tasks, to persuade other family members to share some of the work load, and to make the schedule as efficient as possible.

Spiritual Dangers

Self-pity. Many women are prone to the sin of self-pity. They feel that their lives are more difficult than others': they use their mental energies imagining what their lives could be like, if only . . .

Women who indulge in self-pity fail to comprehend God's sovereignty in their lives. They don't realize, or don't wish to realize, that God controls all circumstances. Counting blessings is a helpful exercise, but not usually successful unless accompanied by a recognition of the sinfulness of self-pity and a positive determination to eliminate it with God's help.

Resentment. This is closely related to self-pity. Both concentrate on wrongs (often imagined or exaggerated) done to the individual. Resentment takes the form of bitterness and resistance to circumstances; it assumes that God did not know what He was doing when He allowed certain things to happen and prevented others from happening. Again, as with self-pity, resentment must be recognized as sin and consciously eliminated from the thought patterns.

Envy. This sin is especially acute when a woman is a "housekeeper" and not a "homemaker." Then the emphasis is on things instead of people. In a materialistic society, a focus on possessions is doubly dangerous for a Christian. There is a danger for envy to creep in when comparisons are made about personal appearance, capabilities, and gifts.

Every woman must have a clear perspective of who she is, of her gifts and talents, and of her capacities and limitations. Some things can be changed. If you are too heavy, diet. If you are lazy, work. But if you are too tall (in your estimation), accept the fact and have the assurance that God knew what He was doing when He made you. If you have a physical limitation that cannot be changed, accept it and find ways to live fully in spite of it. Comparisons with the circumstances of others always lead to problems. Envy and jealousy are two destructive sins: don't fall into their trap.

Complaining. The aforementioned spiritual dangers can be hidden with no outward evidence. But after they have taken root in the heart and flourished there for a while, they inevitably emerge and are reflected in a barrage of bitter complaints. "Better is a dry morsel and quietness with it than a house full of feasting with strife" (Prov. 17:1). Do you often feel a complaint straining to be voiced? Learn to direct that complaint quickly to the Lord instead of your family, and ask Him for a thankful spirit.

Materialism. Many Christian women devote their time to selecting, obtaining, and maintaining possessions in their homes. Their security and self-esteem come from a houseful of modern (or antique, as the case may be) furniture and appliances. It is all going to "rust and burn." We need to be very careful that we don't give our lives to things instead of people, that we don't devote our energies to the accumulation of possessions instead of the practice of the Christian life.

Priorities, Time, and Schedules

Every person in the world is given twenty-four hours a day. Why do some people seem to accomplish so much, and others so little? It all depends on their view of time. Do you see your time as a valuable asset that you can manage and control? Or is time an elusive, fleeting thing, always beyond your grasp?

Do you have specified goals for your housekeeping, your personal development, your family? Do you have plans for wisely using your time to meet those goals?

If you do not yet order your time with a pencil and paper, begin now. You may have an organized and effective memory, but it can't compete with a well-organized schedule for detailed planning of time.

Perhaps you consider yourself a free spirit who works by mood and inspiration, not by schedule. Strangely enough, the right moods strike too seldom. More often, procrastination becomes habit, and goals are never met.

A schedule was never meant to bind and restrict, but rather to free. If a task is placed into the schedule, it will be done sometime: if not today, then tomorrow or next week. It will be accomplished, not forgotten.

Begin by jotting down several goals you would like to meet. Here are possible suggestions:

- Wallpaper a room.

- Read two books this week to the children.
- Do a Bible study in Colossians.
- Plant petunias by the front walk.
- Visit Mrs. Smith in the hospital.

In order to draw up a schedule properly, collect all the necessary information. Keep a calendar near your telephone to record *all* social commitments, medical appointments, and school and church functions for the entire family. Keeping a small notebook in your purse enables you to jot down any relevant information when you are away from home. A tablet in a convenient place at home records random thoughts about projects, ideas, work that relates to your house, and family and personal interests. The ten seconds you spend writing down these ideas will pay big dividends in seeing your goals accomplished. Such a list might look like this:

- Coffee table leg scratched — check hardware for cover.
- Write letter to Grandma.
- Call bookstore — check for new book.
- Make dental appointments.
- Check on crochet classes.

These are not urgent items, but should merely be noted for including later in an organized schedule.

After collecting all the available information, draw up a weekly schedule. A form can be purchased at any stationery store. After experimenting for several years I developed my own (figure 3), which I get printed inexpensively at a local shop in quantities of fifty or so. You could easily sketch one each week on a sheet of paper.

In using such a form, first include all mandatory items such as appointments. Then schedule your work. You may have an established routine and not need to write every duty on the schedule. If you are just beginning to use a schedule, include *everything* you want to get done. Be sure to schedule time for Bible study, physical exercise, serious reading, and hobbies. Such items will occasionally be crowded out by pressing family demands, but they are more likely to be accomplished if they are listed.

	Morning	Afternoon	Evening
Saturday			
Friday			
Thursday			
Wednesday			
Tuesday			
Monday			
Sunday			

Figure 3

Many women such as I prefer to schedule heavy-housework days a few times a week, leaving the other days open for personal interests, church activities, and family times.

Remember that you must be flexible. If your child is ill or needs listening to and counsel, that should take precedence over cleaning the bathroom. If a friend experiences a family emergency, you may want to delay papering the bedroom walls to prepare a meal to take to her home. If your husband wants to discuss a job change, by all means delay the dusting. Keep in mind that if it is on the schedule, it is under control. If you don't finish it this Tuesday, do it next Tuesday.

The needs of people, especially in your own family, always come before the needs of a house. Note the word *needs*. Children occasionally make unreasonable demands: a gentle explanation with an interesting alternative activity can occupy the time of a fretful, obstinate child. At one time I had three preschool children at home. If I talked on the phone for very long, they would begin to demand my attention. I collected a number of interesting items and kept them near the phone: blocks, crayons, scissors, coloring books, small plastic animals — all items that would occupy their attention near me, yet allow me to finish a conversation. I gave them these toys only when I talked on the phone, so the children came to view them as a privilege.

Your work is important. Supporting and encouraging productive human beings is a satisfying occupation. Few working people have the opportunity to see others reach their full potential as human beings through their efforts. That is the fulfillment of a homemaker.

CHAPTER 10

THE WORKING WOMAN

PAT WORKED until shortly before the birth of her first child. Eleven years later, after the youngest of her three children entered school, she returned to a secretarial job. She felt that the "extra money" would be helpful, though her husband received adequate wages. The first few weeks were hectic as Pat learned her work responsibilities and tried to balance her time between her job, her husband, her children, and the housework. She was perpetually fatigued, but felt that once she found the balance between home and work, she would feel better. Still, months went by, and though she learned the job well, Pat never found time to schedule all the activities she considered essential. She struggled with the situation for a year, finding the job becoming more monotonous, her children more rebellious, and her husband bewildered. Finally she quit, feeling she had been a failure, but unable to continue in the situation.

Ann was twenty-eight, unmarried, an excellent secretary, and frustrated. She had completed a two-year secretarial course with honors and for eight years had worked for the personnel director of a large company. She knew she was efficient and capable and had the complete trust of her boss, but she was also aware that she had climbed her career ladder about as far as she could go. She knew the job well, and while it pleased her to do excellent work, few new challenges confronted her. She had had a succession of roommates, some she hardly remembered. She attended a church with strong Bible teaching, but few single adults; most of them helped in the children's department of the Sunday school and seldom interacted socially. She felt at peace about the fact that, at least for the present, it was God's will for her to be single; though she dated occasionally, no permanent relationships seemed to develop. If anyone had asked Ann to characterize her life, she probably would have said "lonely."

The very title of this chapter is a paradox. All women work — work hard. Whether they are homemakers, employees in business, or both, they put many hours and much effort and energy into their tasks.

Admittedly we issue some cautions about the difficulties facing working mothers, and we stress the importance of a woman's influence in her home. Yet we must face reality. A third of the United States working force are women. For a multitude of reasons, women are becoming more involved in jobs of all kinds. Single women work to provide for their own needs and to pursue a profession; widows and divorcees work to provide a living for their families; wives work to have extra money for their families and to fulfill a creative need. And as they work, they are, in general, still underpaid, unrecognized, and perhaps unfulfilled.

How can a woman make the best of a working situation? A single woman can apply this entire book to her life, since she has fewer family responsibilities than a married woman. Yet she encounters troublesome issues as she labors in what is historically man's domain. For all women, there are conflicts and pressures that must be met with positive answers.

Are there illegitimate, wrong reasons for a woman to work? Yes, and here are a few:

● Escape from the home. One married woman said, "I can't stand to be a home all day. Housework is so boring, and the kids drive me up the wall. I work just to get out of the house."

• More money for luxuries. Another woman said, "My husband has gone as far as he can in his company. He's too old to quit his job and look for other work. I'm working so I can have some of the good things that he can never give our family. I want to move to a better house, and for once, we're going to go someplace exciting for our family vacation."

• Status. To many women, status comes with a nice home and material advantages. In this day of women's liberation it also results from certain freedom, activities, and positions. But real security comes only from God and not from any position of employment. Holding a job to gain status or material advantage or position will lead to frustration and failure.

Another caution: When children are in their formative years, it is wise for a mother to consider working only in an extreme situation. The training and character development of a child are responsibilities given by God to parents, and only in serious circumstances should they be delegated to others. If a husband and wife together decide that the mother must work, a careful search should be made to provide proper care for the children: not someone who will "look after" a child, but a trusted individual who has the same principles and goals and standards as the parents, someone willing to teach and train the child when the parents are absent. Titus 2:4,5 teaches that "young women" are to be "workers at home" and to "love their children." This verse reflects the value of maintaining one major responsibility (the home) when children are young.

Advantages and Benefits

Financial profit. Without question, most women work to have more money. The need may be crucial, as in the case of the single woman, the divorcee, or the widow; or the pay may contribute to the betterment of the family or survival in "hard times." Money as an end in and of itself, or as a means for acquiring more "things," is an improper motive for working. Wages that help fulfill a genuine need are honorable.

Claire exemplifies the woman whose income is essential. She is in her early forties with two children approaching college age. Three years ago her husband was seriously injured in an industrial accident. Although he receives some financial compensation, Claire returned to work to bolster the family budget and to secure a college education for their children. The experience unified the family as they discussed and decided together that Claire should find a job and that her husband and children would carry the load of housework.

This illustration raises a key point. If a married woman works outside the home, her husband should be willing to shoulder a significant share of the housework. When single women share a residence, they should equitably share in the efficient functioning of that household.

Use of gifts or natural talents. A young secretary we know has been married three years, has no children, and finds holding a job a profitable use of her time. She is intelligent, organized, and efficient. She frequently evaluates what is best for her, her relationship with her husband, and her home. To this point, she has continued working.

Many women are suited to particular work and find their abilities used fully in their jobs. Women who enjoy contact with people can become good teachers, receptionists, nurses, salespersons, missionaries, or civic leaders. Women who like work involving details may desire to be accountants, secretaries, writers, or musicians.

Before taking a job, a woman should evaluate her capacity, her interests, and her abilities, then search for the appropriate work. There are many aptitude tests that can give counsel toward a particular field.

Contact with people. Working provides opportunities for association with others that can be socially and intellectually stimulating. There may be opportunities for relationships that will lead to evangelism or helping people to grow to Christian maturity. Working gives a sense of involvement in the real world: but do not rely completely on your co-workers for this involvement. Often employment relationships are temporary and transitional, and lasting relationships don't develop on the job. Satisfying and fruitful friendships should also be formed in your neighborhood and church.

Maximum use of time. Working women are forced to

structure their schedules and use their time to bring the most benefit to themselves, and to their families if they are married. One young wife told me, "If I didn't have a job, I would sleep until noon and never get anything done. It helps me get going in the morning and organize my time." You must consider what is important to include in your schedule and what is nonessential.

Problems of Working Wives and Mothers

Fatigue. Most working wives find themselves caught in the crunch between their jobs and their homes. Christian women want to perform well in both situations, but often find the combination exhausting and live on the thin edge of chronic fatigue.

A young working woman said, "Since I instituted a daily and weekly planning time, I usually have *time* to get things done. My problem is that I often lack the energy. If I carry out my planned schedule, many times I end up exhausted."

This problem has to be met by incorporating the help of other family members, cutting back on working hours, lowering housekeeping standards, dropping outside activities, or quitting the job altogether.

Boredom. Despite recent publicity about joining the work force to find "fulfillment," very few truly stimulating and energizing jobs exist, especially for women. Many jobs are routine to the point of monotony, offering little or no opportunity for creativity.

One way to battle this disadvantage is to do the best possible work at all times, maintaining a standard of excellence that will provide a measure of challenge. Keep Colossians 3:23 continually in mind, making service to Christ the motive for your work.

More importantly, boredom frequently has a root of doubt and questioning whether we are in God's will. If you are convinced that God has directed you to work and has provided the job, you have a sense of purpose that will do much to eliminate boredom in even the most routine of jobs.

Time pressures. Christian women want to maintain good family relationships and participate in spiritual activities even when they hold down full-time jobs. They also want to keep high standards in their homes. Pressures inevitably result, such as —

    — how much time with family members?
    — how much time for personal interests?
    — how much time for housekeeping?
    — how much time at church functions?

The list goes on. You must make frequent evaluations and adjust the use of time accordingly. What are the essential requirements on your time? What can be eliminated? Should something be added that is now missing? You can begin a schedule evaluation by blocking out the hours between the time you leave home for work and the time at which you return. Then block out the hours you sleep. The rest is discretionary time. You must then place into your schedule all the things necessary for your personal and family needs.

If you are married and have a family, determine the needs of each family member and how they can be met and the time that will take. Include such things as children's extracurricular activities, recreation and devotions with the family, church commitments, social endeavors, and special family interests. At the bottom of the list, evaluate how much housekeeping you should do, and wherever possible reduce that work load. Consider personal standards: are they too exacting for the schedule you keep, the life-style you lead, the ages of your children? Train other family members and draw help from them. Conserve your energy for people rather than housework.

Under pressure resulting from working and homemaking, it is essential to maintain a program of personal interests — that is, to keep spiritually, mentally, and physically whole. When pressures are heavy, it is easy to neglect the activities that develop us as persons. Carefully guard a time each day for personal fellowship with God — Bible reading and prayer. That crucial time will flavor your relationships for the rest of the day. Include time in the schedule for an activity that is particularly for you — perhaps an exercise group, a painting class, voice lessons, an evening class at a local college, craft sessions, or volunteer hospital work.

Materialistic outlook. Most people in the working world are motivated by a materialistic approach to life. As Christians, we need to guard against this subtle trap. Know clearly the reasons why you want to earn money. Keep a detailed account of your expenditures to discover if your objectives for your wages are being met. Attempt to live modestly rather than extravagantly.

Negative effect on the family. There is a danger that a woman's absence from the house during her working hours can have a bad effect on her family life. Husbands may be resentful of her full schedule and apprehensive about their children's care. The children may feel unrestrained and uncared for and, also, imposed upon if they are required to shoulder more responsibility than they can handle emotionally. It is possible, too, that if a Christian woman cannot handle the two roles well — homemaker and working woman — she may emphasize achievement in the more public aspect of work and neglect the first responsibility God has given her.

Spiritual Dangers

Do you keep spiritually fit in spite of the pressures of your job? Are you careful to recognize sin as it enters your life and to deal with it completely? Evaluate periodically the totality of your life and where your job fits into the objectives God has for you. There are a few problems that can creep in.

Complaining. It is common to hear people complain about their jobs, their boss, the company, the conditions, or their co-workers. Much of the grumbling is based on fact — inequities do exist — and it is easy for a Christian to join the steady stream of complaints. Christian women, whether in or out of the home, need to keep Philippians 2:14 always in mind: "Do all things without grumbling or disputing."

Resentment. Unless we accept adverse circumstances as an unavoidable condition of life, resentment will flood in. Some women resent their particular job: the pay is too low, the boss too demanding, the working conditions too difficult. Other women resent having to work at all. Perhaps their husbands are incapable of working or receive wages too low to meet the minimum family requirements. Guard against directing resentment against other people. God has ordered your circumstances; accept them from Him.

Guilt. Many working wives, especially if they have children, simply cannot find the time to accomplish all they feel they should do at work, at home, and with their families. They move through life in a fog of guilt, wishing they could be more or do more. You must recognize your limitations, accept them, and live within them. If God has clearly directed you to take a job, and you and your husband feel confident about that decision, then press ahead in your work and never feel guilty about the things you simply cannot do.

Adapting to the world's mold (temptation). A young secretary said, "It's a real struggle to keep my eyes on the Lord when I'm exposed to the world's thinking and value system. It's a test of faith which I sometimes fail."

Working daily with non-Christians brings Christians under pressure to succumb to their values and world views. It takes a daily commitment to God and a strong faith to resist the temptation to conform.

Pat married while very young. When her two children were still toddlers, she started to work as a salesclerk in a large store. Her husband was a bus driver. She was intelligent and capable and quickly advanced to buyer and then to department manager; her husband remained in his same job. Pat began to experience a vague embarrassment when introducing him to her new associates. After a few years she developed an interest in another buyer, divorced her husband, and remarried. Pat was a Christian, but allowed the world's thinking patterns to become her own.

Problems of Single Working Women

The single working woman faces problems unique to her circumstances. The world of the single working woman differs significantly from the married woman's by the absence of family responsibilities associated with husband or children. Although a single man also encounters crucial problems, he does not face the complexity of opinions and situations that confront single women.

Competition for careers. Single women must approach their jobs as though they plan to remain for an extended length of time. This means that they want jobs with challenge, opportunities for advancement, and fair salary. In a traditionally male realm, competition is keen for the better positions. It is difficult for many women to summon the aggressiveness needed to meet the struggle for advancement. Not all single women want a competitive environment or advancement, but unless they have some special skill or level of competence, job security is endangered. As a single working woman you must learn to live confidently in a competitive environment even though you may not be by nature a competitive person.

How should you as a woman respond to the demands and circumstances of competition? The statements on competition in chapter 4 will be helpful, but these may be added:

1. Resolve before God any bitterness or resentment that may have built up as a result of competition.

2. Determine whether you are a competitive person, and if so, in what ways.

3. Commit your position and your job to God in prayer.

4. If you are not competitive in the sense of trying to gain new responsibilities, then concentrate on proficiency and excellence in your current duties. Compete only against your own standard for yourself. Set specific goals for personal improvement and proficiency.

5. If you are a competitive person and wish to gain responsibility or a new position, you must be both proficient where you are and train yourself for increased responsibility. Before you compete, be sure that you have the ability to do the desired job. Only frustration will result if you obtain the goal and cannot produce.

6. Do not compete against your co-workers, but only against your own or the company's standards. Personal competition can be emotionally destructive and disastrous for relationships.

7. You may work in circumstances where there is a strong male partiality for any promotion. As a Christian you may need simply to accept this limitation and do the best you can rather than arm yourself for battle to change the system. God is in charge of your life and job (Ps. 72:6,7).

8. Finally, do not give your life and emotional energy to

something that does not ultimately count. Place job and position in the perspective of God's total plan for your life. Reaching people with the gospel is far more important than career advancement.

The constant pressure of decision making. As a single woman, you probably have no other person to whom you can consistently turn for help and support when making decisions. In marriage there is (or at least should be) constant dialogue on a full range of problems, but the single woman must make all her own judgments. Yes, there are roommates and friends who can offer counsel, but they bear none of the ultimate consequences of the decisions. Only you can carry that responsibility.

Certainly women can develop expert decision-making ability. But many women tire of the constant pressure of that process, especially in terms of finances, automobiles, insurance, home repairs, and myriad other matters historically relegated to men. When pressure and discouragement are at a height, there may be no one around to offer refuge.

Yet God has put you in these circumstances and provides what is needed to live joyfully and contentedly. "Seeing that His divine power has granted to us *everything* pertaining to life and godliness, through the true knowledge of Him who called us by His own glory and excellence" (2 Peter 1:3). God has certainly put you in a place where *He* is your only source of strength and provision — but you must draw upon that source. The ultimate issue is your relationship to God both in salvation and in daily living.

If this pressure concerns you, review the discussion in chapter 2 and especially consider these factors:

1. Make sure you are developing a daily devotional life in which your focus is on your relationship to Christ. He is your only source of strength, so do not cut off that source.

2. Develop a few close friendships with single women who have spiritual depth. Avoid a rapid succession of roommates. Deep relationships are basic to happiness.

3. Foster good communication with your parents whenever possible. They can give valuable counsel.

4. Develop friendships with one or two married couples

who are genuinely concerned for your welfare. There are many couples who would take an interest in helping in mechanical and financial matters. The friendship should be primarily with the wife to avoid problems of questionable relationships.

5. Do not be afraid to ask for help and counsel when you have a genuine need. Many do not offer help simply because they are unaware of any need.

6. Take it upon yourself to learn basic skills of finance control and home repairs. You probably can do much more in these matters that you think.

The marriage issue. Society — and especially Christian society — makes the single man or woman painfully aware of his or her "deficiency" in not being married. Thus, even when the issue of marriage has been prayerfully committed to God, it is constantly surfaced by others.

Few women do not desire marriage, and few are closed to the possibility. Yet there are many godly women whom God has led to be single, at least for the time being. First Corinthians 7 certainly authenticates the legitimacy of the single state. Single women can make a special contribution to the body of Christ and have an unusual devotion to Him (1 Cor. 7:32-35). A godly single woman is far better off than an unhappy wife in a marriage of desperation. The church has much to learn in this regard.

Yet you must face reality. There are pressures from many directions. There are certainly frequent questions and desires from within a single Christian woman. If you desire marriage, you should pray for a husband, but that desire must not control you. God has a significant contribution for you to make now that cannot be made in marriage. Do not thwart His plans by that restless impatience that prevents you from doing God's will now. Commit the timing and possibility of marriage to God: you are His, and He wants the best for you. Then you will need to recommit it each time you sense the marriage issue beginning to control your thoughts and dominate your prayers.

In a society of Christians in which marriage is the norm and singleness is viewed as the exception, it takes a deeply committed woman to remain in the midst as a victorious Christian rejoicing in her state and calling. But God's grace is sufficient here, too (2 Cor. 9:8).

Moral pressures in the working environment. For a Christian single woman, the moral pressures of the work environment can discourage or tempt to great extremes. Crude language, dirty jokes, and sexual innuendos must be faced by all Christians. But the impact seems especially heavy on a single woman, since to many she is "fair game." The pressure comes not only from men, but from other women who have succumbed to immoral relationships. The surest protection from such pressures is a consistent walk with God. These guidelines may prove helpful:

1. Make your stand as a Christian known.

2. Do not give your approval to improper or immoral actions or statements.

3. Voice your disapproval of crude language or jokes. You can politely and sincerely say, "Mr. Henry, I'd really appreciate it if you would not swear so much. I know you have the right to do it, but it really makes my job difficult." If you are a good employee, that will carry a lot of weight.

4. In some instances you may have to quit your job if the moral situation becomes unbearable.

5. Dress tastefully, not provocatively. Do not encourage advances in any way. Avoid idle flirtation. It is impossible for moral impurity to result without mutual encouragement.

6. Remember that no job is worth compromising your convictions.

7. Committed Christians can change the environment of an office, so be a part of the solution to the moral problem.

8. Try to develop genuine friendships with non-Christian women in your job. Moral pressure and crude language will come from them, and honest friendship will help influence them and alleviate the problem.

Opportunity. No matter what laws are passed or what court decisions are made, employment opportunities for most women remain limited. For single women who *must* have employment, this can be distressing. Often pay is not as high for a woman as for a man doing the same job. It is at this point that the Christian single woman faces a dilemma, one she may face for life. How she responds will largely determine her response to a multitude of future life problems: if she becomes bitter and resentful, she will carry it into her Christian life and witness; if she responds with hatred and radical political activity, she will be deterred from the goal God has set for her; if she accepts the circumstances and seeks to effect change by competence and Christian witness, she will at least be able to influence the status of others where she works and at the same time clearly share Christ.

Acceptance. There is little place in most churches for single women over twenty-five. The only group in harder straits is divorcees. Yet all of us have a desperate need for acceptance — who we are, how God made us, and where He has placed us. For a single woman, acceptance deeply involves a measure of social involvement.

Whether single, divorced, married, or widowed, you should consider your job an opportunity from God — to serve Him, to serve others, and to mature spiritually.

CHAPTER 11

THE MILITARY AND
GOVERNMENT EMPLOYEE

GEORGE HAD just returned from two months of temporary duty overseas. It had been a strenuous time: his job was tough, the hours long, and his relationships with supervisors strained. Remembering his past reunions with his wife and family after such separations, he was greatly anticipating arriving home. But instead of joyously welcoming him home, as he expected, his wife was discouraged and crying. The family was upset, and the children undisciplined.

Together they sat down and reviewed what was happening. She was tired of being the head of the family in his absence. The pressure of having total supervision of the children was draining her emotionally.

As they discussed the situation, they remembered that in the first two years of their military career they moved three times. In the last eight years they moved four times. His job schedule was erratic and demanding, and the pressures were heavy. Yet the job needed to be done. They were both convinced that God had called them to a career in the military and that He had given them a significant ministry among their friends. In fact, several had come to know Christ, and George and his wife were looked upon as spiritual leaders in their military community. They were confident that God would give them answers to the problem, but they wondered what could have been done to prevent such a crisis.

Others have faced similar problems and crises. In this chapter I focus primarily on the military, both because of my extensive personal experience in the armed forces, and also because it is a distinct segment of American society. If you are a civilian employee of the armed forces, I suggest that you also study the chapters that deal with your particular type of job (salaried, hourly, or professional).

In many ways the military is a cross section of our entire society. People come from all levels of education, abilities, skills, and backgrounds. There are significant differences between the enlisted, noncommissioned, and commissioned officers. The Army, Navy, Air Force, and Marines — each has various distinctions. There are differences in types of duty, jobs, and work environments. Yet, with all these variations, many aspects of life are common to all military personnel, and we can isolate some specific problems and perhaps give some significant help.

Advantages and Benefits

Variety. You will find variety in assignment and in location. It is generally possible to change career fields once, or even twice, in the course of a military career. Even while doing the same kind of work, the different locations and circumstances make the job interesting and appealing. No two assignments will seem the same.

Security. Military and government employment offers significantly more security than most civilian jobs. If you are doing satisfactory work, you can almost be assured of finishing a career. Officers can expect more scrutiny than enlisted men; they have more career risks because of an "up or out" promotion system. But only in times of severe reduction in forces due to mandatory cutbacks will people be removed against their will from the military. Civil service jobs are slightly less secure, but still offer more stability than most civilian employment.

Travel. The military offers the opportunity to live in many parts of the United States and in many foreign countries. For those who like change and variety, this is an excellent way to fulfill that desire. Travel and change can prove beneficial to a family as they move and adjust together. Children who have been exposed to other cultures and new experiences are often more tolerant, more capable, and more sophisticated than the majority of their peers.

Pay and benefits. In recent years the pay in the military services and civil service has been equivalent to pay in civilian jobs of comparable difficulty and training requirements. Many servicemen receive specialized training that will benefit them vocationally when they leave the military. The significant retirement plan available after only twenty years of service is a determining factor for many. After a career of twenty years, a serviceman can retire and receive half of his base pay. Because pay has increased in recent years, many of the side benefits have decreased, but some are still significant — especially, free medical care for the family.

New spiritual starts. Each transfer to a new job or location brings the opportunity for a new start. In spiritual matters it is often easier to build a new reputation and develop new influence rather than live down past performance. If you have "blown it" in one location, you will have an opportunity to begin anew. Also, if you are unable to find the Christian fellowship in one location, it may be available elsewhere. Witnessing with results may be easier in some places than others.

Disadvantages and Restraints

Joe entered the Army at age eighteen and remained for thirty years. During that time he moved fourteen times to locations all over the world. On his second assignment he met and married a girl who had lived in one town — indeed, in one house — all her life. She was never able to adjust to the emotionally wrenching experience of making friends and leaving them, setting up housekeeping over and over again, and seeing her children moved from one school to another. She became bitter and withdrawn, and her attitude was reflected in their sons. Joe was bewildered. He found fulfillment in his work but despair at home, and he felt powerless to correct the situation.

Frequent moves. Although Joe's experience is an exaggeration of most military careers, one crucial disadvantage of a military job is the frequent moving. Pulling up roots, disengaging friendships, establishing new educational patterns for the children, and resettling in a new home can have an unstabilizing effect on the family if each move is not carefully planned and positively approached. These demands make the family unit all the more important: home must be where the family is. Chapter 5 provides further help.

Security. Although financial and job security can be a significant advantage in some cases, it may present a temptation to "walk by sight and not by faith." The attitude that our needs are met by the government rather than God Himself is all too easy to adopt. An overriding concern for financial security can paralyze a person's ability to see God's direction if God should lead to a new circumstance. True security can never be found in a job, but only in God.

Separation from the family. Most certainly the military will require times of separation from the family. In some cases it could entail as much as 15 or 20 percent of a career. These separations may last from a few days to a full year on an isolated or remote assignment. No one enjoys these separations, but they can do a great deal to deepen relationships and dependency on God. On the other hand, separations can have a negative effect on the family. If a marriage is not solid, a long separation can be disastrous. Separation has the greatest effect on the children, since their relationships are more tenuous and dependent on frequent contact. It also can place unbiblical authority and responsibility on a wife.

Job dissatisfaction. There will inevitably be times when the military job is not enjoyable or fulfilling. This may be especially true in the enlisted ranks. Morale can be a problem unless the job is meaningful. And the morale problem is even more common in a peacetime army. A competitive, ambitious person will have difficulty in routine, dull work unless his attitude is right. In the military, griping and complaining are often accepted as the norm. You generally cannot choose your job, so accepting what is assigned can lead to dissatisfaction.

War. Life in the military is not just "another" job. War is always a possibility, and in much of our history, a reality. Danger threatens. Separations can be long. A soldier must have biblical convictions on the issue of the Christian's relationship to war.

Lack of freedom. In several aspects of the military there is considerable lack of freedom. Future assignments or jobs are determined by others. Work schedules may include twenty-four-hour days. Many job schedules are irregular and demanding. Resigning from the military may not be an option, because commitments must be fulfilled.

Spiritual Dangers

The military is not unique in presenting barriers to spiritual development. Your own maturity and commitment will determine your spiritual growth. But there are key dangers that officers and enlisted personnel face. Here I highlight a few in each category.

For enlisted personnel:

Bitterness. Bitterness and sarcasm can develop quickly in adverse circumstances. The military has a strong class and rank structure that might make an enlisted person feel inferior. But this happens in other segments of society where differences are created by job classifications, living environments, and income brackets. The Christian must carefully guard his attitude and response to circumstances and incidents that can generate bitterness.

Job opportunity. There is less opportunity for advancement in both pay and position for the enlisted person. If he is ambitious and wants to become an officer, he is limited after a certain age. Some jobs and responsibilities are unavailable to him. Certain career fields may be closed and opportunities for promotion limited.

Focus on security. Many people enter the military without intending to make it a career. Suddenly they find themselves at a ten-year point and remain in the service simply because of the security. This focus can be an entirely wrong motivation for remaining in a particular job. If a person does not have a marketable skill, a "fear" of the outside world can develop. At this point the individual must establish his security in God and be convinced of God's will in job location. Then job security assumes a proper perspective.

Laziness. In many jobs, a man can avoid putting in a full day or making a wholehearted effort. Sometimes indolence is an accepted practice among workers. In that case, when someone does work hard, there is strong peer pressure because the standards of a competent, conscientious person point up the failures of others. Don't get caught in the trap of being lazy or yielding to peer pressure: it will damage your testimony and hurt your opportunities for promotion. Because it is not easy to fire a person from the military, job motivation has suffered. As a Christian you must rise above the temptation to be lax. Laziness in your job will be reflected in every aspect of your life.

Griping. One of the classic images of a military person is the constant complainer: he gripes about his job, his supervisor, his pay, his privileges, his location. In the Scriptures we are told to "do all things without grumbling or disputing" (Phil. 2:14). Griping always has a negative influence on morale. It can destroy a good testimony. The Christian is obligated to have a positive influence and to look for what is good. Complaints lead ultimately to bitterness, not just against the system, but against God.

Justifiable criticism expressed in proper places is certainly not griping. Passivity helps no one, but positive action to correct wrongs makes a beneficial contribution. A griping Christian rarely has a vital walk with Christ. And what's more, grumbling will infect others — fellow workers, other Christians, and your family.

Peer pressure. The enlisted person, more than the officer, seems to be afflicted with peer pressure to conform. He feels the pressure to drink, to gripe, to be involved in immorality just because everyone else is doing it. The housing facilities, especially for a single man or woman, are often barracks or dormitories where everyone sees and knows what you do. This pressure diminishes considerably after marriage, when you maintain separate quarters.

The problem of peer pressure must be met in the same way we meet every other pressure to adapt to the world's system: we actively determine, by God's help, not to be conformed to the image of the world (Rom. 12:2).

For officers the spiritual dangers are:

Pride. It is a subtle trap to believe that you are better than someone else because of your position or rank. (Pride is essentially the idea that "I am better than someone else.") Rank exists as an orderly means of accomplishing a job — not for giving status or authority outside the context of that job. For the Christian officer, there is no place for conceit or arrogance. You have your commission by the grace of God, and it places you in a position to bring glory to God and to share a clear witness before others. A realistic and proper use of your position is the only way to have that kind of testimony.

Ambition. The officer corps can be highly competitive, since promotions are based on superior performance. Some find it difficult to leave promotion in God's hands and to do the job excellently only for God's glory. It is easy to structure your entire career on the concept of "filling the blocks" so that you can attain high rank. When you put career first and your family, spiritual responsibilities, and ministry are neglected, disaster will eventually occur. But if you have done your work well and place your relationship with God and your family first, you can leave promotion in God's hands.

Neglect. Neglecting the family can be a major problem for a person who is highly dedicated to his job and pushing for recognition and promotion. Even without that kind of ambition, there are heavy job requirements that may cause you to focus on survival in the system rather than on your family. You need imagination and flexibility to keep proper perspectives and priorities as the family's needs change.

Spiritual depth. Because of his position and rank, an officer may feel that he has equivalent stature in the Christian community. He may be reluctant to admit his spiritual needs and to ask for help in his own walk with God. Someone once ventured the opinion that if a person is a Christian officer, then he is qualified to lead spiritually. Nothing is further from the truth. He may have the ability to lead in the flesh, but lack spiritual depth of life, action, and character to provide spiritual leadership.

Do not allow yourself to be forced into a role of spiritual leadership when you desperately need spiritual growth in your own life. Actively seek out the spiritual help that you need. Develop a knowledge of the biblical principles and conditions for leadership, and refuse to accept such positions until you are spiritually prepared and qualified.

Guidelines and Suggestions

I have made the assumption that you are confident of your being in the will of God in the military or in civil service. You may have only a three- or-four-year commitment, or you may be planning on a long career. In either case God wants you to live *today* and not habitually anticipate retirement or release from service. The best testimony and the most personal satisfaction are achieved by doing an excellent job where you are right now.

Family. Your wife and children must rank high on your list of priorities. Despite irregular schedules or extensive separations, you must be certain that their needs are fulfilled. This requires developing a slightly different concept of the home for your family. Since your geographical location will change, home must be where you are together as a family.

1. Your first priority is your wife. There is great security for children in a home where genuine love is openly expressed between the husband and wife. Howard Hendricks says, "The best thing you can do for your children is to love your wife." Remember that your wife will experience unusual pressures due to your schedule and absences. Though she does not want to be independent, she must learn to be capable in many circumstances. Therefore, when you are home be sure to be the biblical head of your household. Remove as many burdens and pressures as possible from your wife. Many books have been written on biblical marital relationships. I refer you to these: among those I recommend are *I Married You* by Walter Trobisch, *The Christian Family* by Larry Christenson, *Heaven Help the Home* by Howard G. Hendricks, and *How to Be Happy Though Married* by Tim LaHaye.[1] But more important, study your Bible for yourself on this issue. Ephesians 5 is a good starting point.

2. Plan special time with your children as a group and individually. Focus on learning to know them and developing relationships with them. A strong personal bond with your children will sustain your relationship through absences and irregular schedules. Let your wife and children know that they are valued above career. Express it verbally and demonstrate it in your actions. Some practical ideas are to —

— take your children out to lunch or breakfast individually;

— plan a family night when all the family is home;

— let them help you plan special events well ahead of time (hikes, trips, ball games); this gives them a goal to anticipate;

— plan surprise outings. When I had a particularly heavy schedule, my family would plan and prepare a surprise picnic; they would then call me to dinner, usher me to the car, and drive to a nearby park;

— listen to them when they want to talk; otherwise the time will come when they share very little;

— center your vacations on the family. Ask the children what they would enjoy; plan relaxed, fun-filled vacations in which the development of relationships is more important than travel or sightseeing.

3. When you have an irregular schedule or know of impending separations, plan blocks of time with the family. Give them some memorable experiences. The times need not be long. Even a few hours will do. I have not hesitated to take the children out of school occasionally for key family activities.

4. Avoid substituting gifts and material possessions for your presence. Your family wants *you*, not the things your money can buy.

5. When you have an option in choosing a job or assignment, put the needs of your family above your career. Rarely will there be a significant conflict, but your attitude and your expression to the family in this is highly important. When you must have a separation for some period of time, simply accept this as God's will for you and know that God will provide for

both your needs and your family's during your absence.

6. Be involved in your children's activities. Know what they are thinking and feeling. Keep the lines of communication open. Some ways to do this are to —

— extend times at evening meals, especially when the children are in a talkative mood;

— *never* turn down a request by your son or daughter to speak to you privately;

— have devotional times with them individually on occasion;

— apologize and ask their forgiveness when you are wrong or have mistakenly accused or punished them;

— do all you can to be present for functions *they* think are important (choral programs, sports events, parties);

— know what they are doing in school;

— meet their friends. Encourage your children to invite their friends home so that you can observe them in peer relationships.

7. Avoid having your wife hold a job. Your home needs every measure of stability that you and your wife can provide. If she works, it will remove the necessary element of her presence from the family. Material concerns and the desire for a home of your own cannot compare with the value of family stability. This is especially important in the military.

8. When you choose your living location, place the family's needs first. Financial investment or material comfort should not be the prime motive in residential location. Carefully consider the neighborhood and the schools as well as the commuting time to your job. For convenience, many find it an advantage to live on the base or post.

Witness. God has given you a great opportunity to have a significant witness to a distinct segment of society. It is difficult for someone outside the military to have a meaningful impact on those within. God has placed you there to be a witness, not merely to do a job. Your testimony will have influence through your words, your actions, your attitude toward your job, your activities, and your relationship to your family. Assured that

God has placed you in your particular situation for His purpose, you should be diligent in getting the training and help that encourages a clear testimony for Christ.

Use your home to witness as a couple. Create an atmosphere in which others are comfortable and know that Christ is honored. In this way your children will also be involved in your ministry. We have found a number of ideas to be helpful, such as —

— having your co-workers to dinner or dessert, occasionally including the children;

— making your home available for social functions. Since we did not drink alcoholic beverages ourselves, we never served them; we sponsored brunches, potluck suppers, and baby showers, and none of these required alcohol;

— beginning a couples' Bible study with non-Christians. An excellent format is a cassette and discussion series called *The Scriptural Home Seminar* by George Sanchez, available from The Navigators;

— having neighborhood barbecues. This is especially good in on-base housing, since people do get to know each other better;

— organizing women's coffees where you have an evangelistic outreach with a speaker on a topic of interest (biblical child rearing, the wife's role in marriage, how we got our Bible, etc.);

— forming a women's morning Bible study.

Fellowship. When you move to a new base, seek out mature Christian fellowship as soon as possible. You need that fellowship for spiritual support and growth, and others need your fellowship. I personally encourage you to give prime consideration to attending the base chapel. When you do that, realize that it would be primarily for outreach to others rather than for your own teaching and training. If God should lead you to be in a civilian church, be sure that you don't abandon a ministry where you work.

Even off base, you will find significant ministry with military people. There are also a number of nondenominational

Christian groups that focus on the military community, and they can provide both training and fellowship: among these are The Navigators, Officers Christian Fellowship, and Campus Crusade for Christ.

In the chapel program there are several effective ways in which you can have an influence. There are always needs for Sunday school teachers for both children and adults. If you develop a strong Bible-centered class, you will gain support; if you try to have an "intellectual" discussion on contemporary issues, it will be weak. Keep it Bible-centered.

Let your evangelical position be known to the chaplains. Do not operate "underground." The chaplains appreciate it and will generally give sufficient freedom. On most bases there are groups such as Men of the Chapel and Women of the Chapel that have monthly meetings. You can have an influence on the speakers and programs.

It is true that you would be more comfortable in your own denomination, but every mission endeavor involves some sacrifice. Certainly the military is a mission field. When your children become teen-agers, you may need to go off base for church. At least you would want to consider a Sunday evening involvement in a local church. It is important for teen-agers to develop firm relationships with Christian peers.

Travel and separation. Frequent or even occasional family separations are never pleasant. But if your relationship with your family is stable, the separation can be a time of strengthening and deepening those bonds. When the relationships are unsatisfactory, separation can be disastrous. How well things go in your absence depends directly on how well they go when you *are* there. You can do several things to make a time of separation a spiritually growing experience for the entire family.

1. As soon as you get to your place of temporary duty or isolated assignment, seek out Christian fellowship as quickly as possible.

2. Set goals for yourself in your personal walk with God — a daily quiet time, Bible study, and witness. You will not be able to minister effectively to your family at a distance unless you are spiritually healthy yourself.

3. Ask God what He wants you to learn during a separation. Together with your family determine some things that God could teach each of you during this time. For instance, your wife could learn greater dependence upon the Lord. The children, as they get older, can accept greater responsibility for needs around the home. Some specific suggestions are to —

— set standards for conduct and discipline for the children before you leave; you are responsible, even when absent;

— assign the children specific responsibilities;

— set spiritual family goals such as a Bible-reading program.

4. Maintain frequent communications by letter and tape recordings. Do not write to your wife and children merely as a group, but also establish individual communication with each member of the family. I suggest that you —

— spend money for telephone conversations if it is financially feasible; the expense is well worth the personal contact;

— give letter-writing high priority;

— write postcards when letters are too time-consuming;

— write each individual in the family on a planned basis;

— use tapes at least monthly;

— send pictures of yourself and what you are doing;

— state specific prayer requests.

5. Make sure the family is well situated and in contact with other Christians during your absence. Ways to do this are by —

— having the family in familiar surroundings where they are comfortable and secure;

— making sure your pastor knows of your absence and checks on the family's needs periodically;

— asking one or two Christian friends to help with the inevitable "fix-it" needs at your house. One of the greatest blessings to my wife in my long absence was a friend who would come over frequently with screw-driver and pliers in hand just checking on things around the house; a plugged toilet or broken window stirs a crisis during a husband's absence;

— doing all you can to get everything in shape before you leave. Fix the car, leave instructions on maintenance, clean the furnace filters, fix the screen door, and check all those other wife-irritants that *will* go wrong in your absence;

— leaving your power of attorney for emergencies;

— making sure your wife has knowledge of your insurance and enough money to pay the bills and meet emergencies without contacting you.

6. Perform as many functions of your role as head of the household, husband, and father as you can from a distance. Share as much of the load with your wife as you can. Counsel the children; be involved in their decisions and their thinking. Instead of buying quantities of trinkets and unique foreign home furnishings, spend the money on communications and contact. However, special gifts for the children and your wife are important. These can be a point of identification with you. I travel a great deal and find that my children really anticipate the small things I bring to them; however, I do not bring gifts every time I travel, and generally they are not expensive items.

7. Contact another Christian couple, a pastor, or someone who will specifically be alert to the special needs of your family in your absence. That is one of the benefits of fellowship in the body of Christ. People express concern for one another and will help in times of need.

Time. Conduct your life on the basis of priorities. In many jobs you will have times of slack and times of intensely heavy work. Use the slack times for constructive purposes — education, Bible study, reading. When you work long hours, you will frequently have additional time off or shorter workdays. Use that time to advantage with the family. Chapter 3 will be especially helpful to a military person.

Job attitude. When jobs, co-workers, and supervisors change frequently, it is imperative that you maintain a positive attitude toward your work. Your reactions to your job and to the mission of your organization will largely determine the effectiveness of your witness. Bitterness, griping, and unhappiness cannot express the joy of knowing Christ to other people. How different are you in your job, your speech, and your actions?

If you are in a kind of military job that is similar to a job type described in another chapter in this book, you can find some helpful guidelines there. I again want to emphasize the necessity of being a committed Christian rather than just an "existent" Christian. The man who is not a committed disciple will encounter many temptations that can cause him to compromise his stand for Christ. That can lead to nothing but unhappiness in your job, personal life, and family. Above all else, make your relationship with God your top priority.

CHAPTER 12

THE SALESMAN

WAYNE KELLEY was a supersalesman. He could sell almost anything: his high school yearbook recorded that Wayne could "sell air conditioners to the Eskimos." For twelve years he worked at various selling jobs — automobiles, office products, insurance, and others. Often he sold for several companies at once. And he made money — lots of it. Everything he touched seemed to turn to gold — except for one thing, his family.

Wayne worked night and day. A customer could reach him twenty-four hours a day, and he would drop everything to make a sale. When friction developed between him and his wife, Wayne at first shrugged it off as a passing phase. Soon he realized that divorce was a real possibility, and he began to panic. For once he couldn't sell himself. They consulted a marriage counselor and a psychiatrist without success. Wayne just couldn't understand it. He gave his children a generous allowance, motorbikes, toys — anything they wanted. They had a large home, a new car every year, and unlimited spending for his wife.

Finally, in desperation Wayne and his wife confided their problems to a neighbor, also a successful salesman, who was known as a "Christian fanatic" in the neighborhood. From this contact Wayne soon realized that they had no spiritual dimension to their lives and that money and success were their gods.

After several weeks of Bible study and friendship, Wayne and his wife confessed their need for a personal Savior and asked Christ to give them eternal life and enter their lives. They felt a new confidence and peace, but soon found that the Bible taught a totally different life-style than the one they lived. They found themselves in a dilemma. Wayne took a step of faith and changed his approach to the job. His Christian neighbor counseled him from the Scriptures that although there would be an initial drop in sales, the changes would make his work even more profitable within a couple of years. Some of Wayne's past sales techniques were ethically questionable. He began to limit his time on the job and lost a few customers.

It was almost as though Wayne's whole world was being turned upside down and rebuilt. Other salesmen put pressure on him because his new and honest approach to selling resulted in fewer sales and made their methods appear unethical. Yet his family was united and happy, so he knew his new life was right. He determined that for the present he would continue the emphasis on his family and the new concept of his job. It wasn't easy to change his life-style, but he was convinced it was the right thing to do.

You may not be a supersalesman like Wayne, but if you are a salesman and a Christian, you have experienced some of his problems. How much should you work? How honest can you be? What if the customer doesn't need or can't afford the product? There are principles and guidelines that can help you to make good decisions. In this chapter I treat sales jobs, which pay on commission or results, such as selling insurance, real estate, industrial products, and services. This does not include regular nine-to-five jobs such as salesclerks or other hourly paid positions.

Advantages and Benefits

For the person who thrives on freedom and people-centered work, a job in sales can bring great satisfaction and fulfillment. There are many benefits in this profession.

Freedom. At some point in life, almost everyone wishes he could be his own boss. As a salesman you can be that in many cases. You have a certain degree of freedom to set your own hours, develop your own customer base, and to work as hard as you like. The only restrictions are specific company requirements and disciplining yourself to make enough money to support your family. Also, the more success you have in sales, the more freedom you have for changing jobs or altering your current job.

Pay proportional to work and ability. Your pay is directly proportional to your effectiveness. No sales, no pay. If you need more money, you work longer and harder. For a person who has good sales ability, there is unlimited opportunity.

People contact. Sales work gives abundant opportunity for contact with people. You have both repeated contact with regular customers and transient contact with one-time customers. You will find unlimited opportunity for witness and friendship.

Disadvantages and Restraints

Yes, disadvantages and restrictions do exist — probably more so in the selling field than in many others. Many people try sales, but few are genuinely successful. It requires a unique combination of ability, personality, and hard work. This list of negatives may seem overwhelming, but it should be taken as motivation for learning and discerning. All these problems have solutions, but they can be destructive if allowed to grow in your life and work.

Pressure. A salesman experiences more pressure to produce than almost any other worker. The pressure comes from two directions: first, the company, with an eye on profits, exerts pressure to sell. A quota may be a requirement for continued employment; second, you must sell enough to make sufficient money to support your family. If you have a difficult time living under pressure and uncertainty, you will be frustrated and unhappy in a sales job. Know your own limitations and abilities. Be careful not to pass this pressure on to your family or to allow it to eliminate personal ministry.

Time. Selling is time-consuming. It is difficult to sell well as a sideline. You must spend time in preparation and studying your product, as well as in actual selling time. The tendency is strong to work excessive hours, either for extra money or just to make enough to live. The less ability you have in selling, the more time it will take you to get the job done.

Ups and downs of business. There are good months and bad months. Rarely are sales and income consistent over a period of time. This means that you must budget carefully and prepare for the low times (which in some businesses may last for several months). Spiritual stability is essential to keep you effective when sales are good and keep you encouraged when sales are bad. During the bad times you tend to work harder and longer to make ends meet; during good times you tend to work harder and longer to seize the opportunity for making more money.

Travel. Many selling jobs involve travel of a few days to several weeks at a time. You may be away from home 50 percent of the time. You must take this into consideration when you think of your family's needs. Plan to use your time with your family effectively when you are at home. Read chapter 11 for specific suggestions on maintaining family stability during periods of separation.

Unusual hours. Many sales jobs occupy odd hours. Selling directly to the customer (e.g., insurance) frequently entails working evenings or on weekends. You must respond to the needs of the customer, so you have little choice as to hours. Therefore your entire schedule with your family and other activities will revolve around a work schedule that is not only unusual, but irregular.

Security. With varying sales success and with pay directly related to sales, security is tenuous. A varying income can be unsettling to many. The security of the job itself is also dependent on your sales success.

Spiritual Dangers

Striving for money. Because your income is directly related to your job effectiveness and because you are free to work as much as you like, desire for money can become a driving force. This temptation is illustrated by a quote from a former salesman: "We were caught up in the American Dream. You've gotta have a house. You've gotta have a country club. You've gotta have two cars. Here you are at ten grand and getting nowhere. So I doubled my salary. I also doubled my grief. I now made $20,000, had an expense account, a Country Squire air-conditioned station wagon given by the company — a wonderful boss. We began to accumulate. We got a house in the suburbs and we got a country club membership and we got two cars and we got higher taxes. We got nervous and we started drinking more and smoking more. Finally, one day we sat down. We have everything and we are poor."[1]

Avoid getting caught in this destructive cycle. Life offers so much more than money or things.

Ethics. In the pressure of trying to make a sale, you can be tempted to shade your ethics. Some people are honest because it will develop good business; others are honest by conviction. As a Christian, it is imperative that you honestly represent your product in the light of your customer's needs. This forces you to sell a product that you can fully endorse, and to avoid selling products to people who neither need nor can afford them. Gullible people are often the easiest targets, so the temptation to take advantage of them can be strong. Perhaps these questions will be helpful to you:

- Is my product worth the price of purchase?
- Do I believe people really need it?
- Am I willing to be honest about my product and the customer's need even if it means losing a sale?

If you can answer yes to these questions, you will have no problem in being an ethical salesman. If not, you may need to reconsider your job or your product. The "just weight" concept of Deuteronomy 25:14,15 applies: "You shall not have in your house differing measures, a large and a small. You shall have a full and just weight; you shall have a full and just measure, that your days may be prolonged in the land which the LORD your God gives you." Also see Proverbs 11:1; 16:11; and 20:10.

Substituting work for family or ministry. Never use your work as an excuse for failing to meet your family's needs or avoiding a spiritual ministry. A common response when a person is asked to be in a Bible study is that he is too pressed with his work schedule to do it. A salesman can easily use this excuse because it is true — selling does take a lot of time. But he also can govern his time more easily. Don't let work keep you from God's basic purposes in your life in regard to your family, spiritual growth, and outreach to others.

Guidelines and Suggestions

Although I have listed several disadvantages, a selling job does present freedom and opportunity to the person who is willing to discipline himself and act on the possibilities. Here are some practical suggestions to make your job as a salesman spiritually productive.

Discipline your time. Unless you learn to discipline your time well, you will never balance your job, family, and ministry without neglecting one or the other. Become an expert in controlling your time both on and off the job. But knowing how is not sufficient: you must do it! Reread chapter 3 carefully and plan specific ways to implement it. Besides the advice in chapter 3, these items are well-suited to your needs:

• Plan your activities a minimum of one week and preferably one month ahead.

• Block out specific time for family and ministry and don't allow the job to encroach on these times.

• Plan your travel and customer contacts at the beginning of each day.

• Don't allow missed or no-show appointments to waste your time; always carry additional work with you.

• Push yourself when you work, but put a limit to the number of hours you work.

Schedule family time. Unless you plan well ahead for family time, it will be neglected. Try to be more available on weekends, especially if you often work at night. Since you have more freedom than hourly or salaried people, try to take days off when your children have school vacations or holidays. Then do something special with them — camping, skiing, swimming, or whatever will make the time special for them.

If I do not take time off and just stay around the house, I usually end up working and not spending time with my children. I need to get away *with* them. I suspect it is the same for hardworking salesmen too.

Know your business. If you do not know your business and product, you can never be a good salesman. Be an expert: don't learn just enough to make a few sales. Know your product and do your homework with the customer's needs in mind; don't waste his time by being ill-prepared. Preparation now will pay dividends in increased sales and saved time.

Avoid "gimmick" sales jobs. Newspapers are filled with sales jobs that seem to offer wealth without work. Frequently the offer is related to items that are questionable in quality, price, or customer need. If the job calls for "gimmick" sales techniques or offers questionable products, be slow to get involved. Such work will generally not be profitable or fulfilling in the long term.

Be a clear witness. In your intense and frequent interaction with people, let it be known that you are a Christian. You should not push or pry, but many will really want to talk about spiritual things. Learn to introduce Christianity through casual conversation, and give others a chance to respond. What if it puts you off schedule on appointments? You would not always have to follow through at that time. Suggest getting together for lunch or an evening talk. The other person will appreciate that, since he has a schedule too. If you are competent in your job, you will more easily win a hearing for the gospel.

What about using gospel tracts? Some use them well, but they stand a distant second to a personal witness. Do you know how to tell others to become a Christian? If not, get help from your pastor, or from any number of books (such as *Winning Ways* by LeRoy Eims and *How to Give Away Your Faith* by Paul Little).

Serve people. If your customers see that you want to serve them, you will have much repeat business. Your motive should be simply to serve. If you serve, you will sell. You may not sell as much at first, but when your reputation is known, you will have ample business.

Remember that you are lumped in with salesmen as a group by most people. They view you with suspicion and mistrust — afraid of "being taken." As a Christian you must break out of this mold. And if you serve, are competent, and wisely share your faith in Christ, you will succeed.

Be objective. As one salesman said, "There is one outstanding characteristic of every good salesman — his eternal optimism."

He was right. A salesman always believes that tomorrow will be better and that sales will increase. He always expects a sale to be closed sooner than it usually is. This optimism is necessary for effective salesmanship, but it can be a hindrance in several ways. Just as he is optimistic about sales possibilities, so is he optimistic about money, time, and family problems. The corrective is to understand this trait and to work at being objective. Try to see things as they really are; compensate for this optimism by being objective in certain key financial and family matters.

CHAPTER 13

THE SELF-EMPLOYED

THE AMERICAN dream of a few decades ago was to have a small family business: to be independent, to be your own boss, to work and be paid directly for your product. With increased industrialization and the growth of large corporations, it has become more and more difficult to operate a small business profitably.

Yet the opportunity remains. Repair shops, small contractors, independent insurance agencies, laundromats, and many other kinds of business are prime examples. People are self-employed as doctors, lawyers, dentists, farmers, and other specialists.

Ron Linden was an expert mechanic. Most of his life had been spent working for others, so he tried self-employment in leasing a service station. But he operated it on the thin edge of financial disaster: Ron had to pay his wholesaler cash, but his business was strained by his customers' outstanding accounts. People needed gas and repairs, so he couldn't say no, but still he had to pay his bills. Finally he sold out and went back to work for someone else as a mechanic.

During this time, Ron and his wife, Karen, began to experience trouble in their lives and marriage. They had undergone problems before, and this was a new flare-up of lifelong struggles. Their children were grown and married, so they seriously considered resolving their problems by divorce. In the midst of this crisis they were confronted with Christ as the answer to their needs. Karen's response was, "My father was an atheist. If he is going to hell, so am I!" Ron's response was indifference and pride: he didn't need outside help. Besides, most people he knew in churches were hypocrites, and he wanted no part of that.

But it became obvious that their needs were beyond help in the human sense. Karen finally received Christ, but struggled in spiritual growth. Ron delayed for three years and finally became a Christian too. After both made commitments, their life together really began to change. They became deeply involved in a church and shared a clear witness of the change Christ brought to their lives.

Almost concurrently with their commitment to Christ came the opportunity to buy the small repair business where Ron was employed. Because of their earlier failure they were hesitant, but after prayer and consideration they finally decided to go ahead. The results were phenomenal. They dedicated the business to God and determined to give generously from the profits. The business grew and prospered. There were new pressures and problems, but they had financial freedom they had never before experienced. The more they earned, the more they gave — even when the financial picture for that month looked bleak. God repeatedly blessed their steps of faith.

What made the difference between their first and second attempts at self-employment? I believe it was their decision to follow God's pattern for their personal lives and their business. God does have much to say about how to conduct business. Several factors are decisive in self-employment.

Advantages and Benefits

Freedom in responsibility. You are your own boss. You have obvious responsibilities, yet you can choose when and how much to work. You have the freedom to choose your employees, to witness on the job, and to limit or expand your work schedule.

Motivation. Most of us are highly motivated when we are "doing our own thing." When the success of the business depends directly on our labor, we are more motivated to perform well and to produce. Whether it is right or wrong, people are always more motivated to promote their own interests than the interests of another.

Finances. If the business is prospering, a self-employed person has greater financial freedom. All profits from the business are his. If he is skilled in the service he is performing, he will always earn more than if he is employed by another. For professional specialists like doctors and lawyers, the prospects of high income are very good.

Security. In the beginning phases of a business or profession, security is limited. However, as a business becomes established, it provides more security than most employment. This is especially important to a person nearing middle age who will find it difficult to obtain employment on the open market.

Family. The entire family can actively participate in many small businesses. Working together can unify a family if they do not become slaves to the business. Making the business succeed becomes an integral part of family life.

While having my car serviced recently, I remarked to the owner of the station on the striking resemblance between him and the boy pumping gas. "That's my son," he answered proudly. "He wanted a motorbike, and he worked here to earn it. 'Course it will be another year before he has his driver's license. For now, we work together. He helps me, and I think he's learning something."

Disadvantages and Restraints

Lack of freedom. This is the other side of the coin. Responsibility brings restriction. You are always on call. You may not be able to leave town any time you like. The customer effectively controls you — especially if business is slow. Even a doctor can't leave town unless his patients are covered by another physician.

Financial pressure. Many small businesses operate on a thin financial margin, especially in the early years. Taxes, rising costs of materials and labor, and the fluctuating economy all bring significant pressure. Profits may be great at times, but losses can prove devastating. A friend of mine was approached by the key employees in his business when it was finally paying off after several years of struggle. They pressed for a profit-sharing agreement. My friend sent them back to their lawyer with the reply, "When you can include a loss-sharing clause, come and see me!" Many people simply do not want the hassle of financial insecurity and would rather not take the risk of self-employment.

Time pressure. In one sense, your time is never your own. You are always obligated to the customer. Your employees do not feel this stress, but you do. You must always be on call. You will face constant pressure to work longer hours and extra days. A mechanic is obligated to respond to his customer's needs; a farmer must harvest at the right time and in the right weather; a storekeeper must keep his shop open at the hours people find it convenient to shop. Time is always in short supply.

Total responsibility. If things go wrong, there is no one else to shoulder the blame. Finances, production, quality, mistakes, and dissatisfied customers all become your problems. That is why a self-employed person deserves the extra profit — for all the responsibility he bears. This is a heavy load, especially when problems develop.

Spiritual Dangers

Overwork. In your own business, extra work can easily replace many important things in your life. Those extra hours can hurt you emotionally, physically, and spiritually. The temptation is strong to "sell your soul to the company store" when it is your own company. Hard work is good; consuming work is wrong. Guard against allowing your own business to deprive you of your family, a spiritual outreach, and your very life.

Pride. As you become successful and more confident in your business, pride may invade your life as you view what *you* have accomplished. At this point remember that all you own and all you have accomplished come from God. What you possess is a trust from God to be used under His direction. You cannot assume credit for the ability He gave you to accomplish your work.

Finances. If you are successful in your self-employed status, you are probably doing well financially. Don't allow money to control and drive you. A rich man was once asked how much money was enough. He replied, "Just a little more." Don't fall into the trap of allowing finances to become an end instead of a means. Chapter 4 provides further guidance on the use of money.

Anxiety. Ulcers seem to be the common denominator of independent businessmen. The total responsibility for success is on your shoulders, humanly speaking, and therefore worry and anxiety can become a way of life. If your self-employment leads to excessive worry, it may be an indication that you should not remain in that circumstance. Fear, worry, and anxiety are paralyzing, both physically and spiritually. First Peter 5:7 says, "Casting all your anxiety upon Him, because He cares for you." Significantly, this verse is preceded by a command for humility and followed by a passage on resisting the devil, standing firm in the faith, and enduring suffering. Your witness shrinks as your anxiety increases, so focus your dependence on God, not yourself. He is your only means of peace and security.

Ethics. As mentioned in the previous chapter, ethics become a key issue when you can set the standards, guidelines, and prices in your work. The Bible stresses the need for ethical business practices, as summarized in Deuteronomy 25:14,15: "You shall not have in your house differing measures, a large and a small. You shall have a full and just weight; you shall have a full and just measure, that your days may be prolonged in the land which the LORD your God gives you." Be careful to give the full value of what you are being paid for. This means that your pricing principle cannot always be "what the market will stand." Jealously guard your honesty and ethics. It is better to lose a little money than to carry a nagging conscience.

Guidelines and Suggestions

Give your business to God. The first step in success as a self-employed person is to give your business to God. How do you do that? In prayer —

— thank God for the business;

— acknowledge to God that the business is His;

— determine to operate on biblical principles and ethics;

— resolve to give to God's work as you are prospered;

— ask God to allow you and your business to be a clear witness for Christ;

— agree to put your family and your walk with Him before the business.

Remember that God does not promise unlimited business success, but He does promise to meet our needs (Matt. 6:33) and bless our lives (Eph. 3:20; Phil. 1:6).

Limit your working hours. You must work hard, but you cannot give your whole life to your work. No business is worth destroying yourself physically, eliminating a spiritual outreach, or neglecting your family.

Guard your family. It is vitally important to guard your family from excessive involvement in the business. Your wife or children must not be forced to give themselves to it inordinately. Don't allow the work to become a wedge in family relationships. Your family deserves far more attention than your business.

Give financially. As God prospers your business, give financially to His work. God's earthly resources are people and material goods. God does operate on a principle of sowing and reaping in every segment of life. If you sow sin, you will reap sin's reward. In 2 Corinthians 9:6, Paul speaks of finances when he says, "He who sows sparingly shall also reap sparingly; and he who sows bountifully shall also reap bountifully."

Use your position. Your position as a self-employed person in the community will bring you admiration and respect. Use that position as an influence for Christ. You have none of the restrictions sometimes imposed by large companies, so you can speak openly and freely on and off the job. Be involved in civic affairs. Influence your community.

Leave your work at work. Owning the business is no reason for it to plague your mind twenty-four hours a day. You must get away from it mentally as well as physically. Develop a hobby and a ministry to others. The pressures are great, but learn to discipline your mind and your time to find relief and relaxation from the job.

A standard of excellence. Know your business thoroughly. Make your work reflect the biblical standard of excellence (Col. 3:23). In applying this standard you need to run your business on sound economic principles. A Christian is not to be an "easy mark" for cheaper performance; but give discounts when it will help your business or when you really want to contribute financially to a group or an individual.

Maintain an attitude of gratefulness for the privilege of owning and operating your own business. Allow God to demonstrate His place in your life by the way you operate day by day in your job.

CHAPTER 14

SPECIAL CIRCUMSTANCES

STEVE'S SCHEDULE was irritating the entire family. His wife was edgy and tense; the children were tired of being quiet during the day, and they resented his absence from their activities. For three years, Steve had worked the swing shift (4 P.M. to midnight). To complicate the situation, it wasn't a Monday-to-Friday job, but rather Wednesday-to-Sunday. Steve left the house at 3:15 P.M. and returned about 12:45 in the morning. He tried to sleep till about 9, but usually the children awakened him. Until recently his wife, Kay, also worked. She left at 8, so there were several days when she and Steve hardly saw each other. Getting the children ready for school was a hassle: Steve didn't want to get up, and Kay was in a frantic rush.

Steve and Kay were Christians and wanted to be effective for God. But with their schedules, they soon started losing touch with people, with the church, and with each other. Their marriage relationship became strained. The children began to complain they didn't feel as if they were really a family. The dilemma was that Steve felt lucky to have his job, and Kay's salary allowed the family to buy a few of the "extra" things.

About three months ago the situation erupted in a heated argument about money. Previous arguments had been about Steve's schedule, his sleep, or who would get the children ready for school. Steve always won — and felt terrible. This time Steve and Kay realized that both were losing. They admitted that they were both slipping spiritually and that the children were suffering. They made some significant changes that have revolutionized their family life. Kay quit her job. Steve reserved every Tuesday night for the family; he started getting up for breakfast with the family on Wednesday and Thursday. Steve and Kay planned to spend specific time together during the week and to give the weekend time to the children. Steve planned Bible study and other projects during the day. The changes revolutionized their lives. In fact, the whole family grew to like Steve's work schedule.

Steve and Kay encountered a special situation. In this chapter on unusual job circumstances, it is difficult to generalize and give categorical guidelines as in previous chapters. I mention only a few general advantages, disadvantages, and dangers. Then I include some specific suggestions in three categories:

- Shift worker;
- Traveler;
- Seasonal worker.

Advantages and Benefits

Unusual time available. Weekday evenings are the most difficult times to use effectively. Therefore, whenever job schedules allow extra days off during daytime hours, you have an opportunity to make good use of the time, since very little else would ever be scheduled in your community, your church, or your family. With good planning, these unusual times can be used to great advantage.

Extra time off. Unless your job is regular shift work, a special schedule frequently allows for extra time off. However, seasonal work is not particularly an advantage unless you can engage in another job. An airline pilot, for example, could develop a business sideline in his flexible time off. Whatever your circumstance, if you get extra time, learn how to use it constructively.

Better pay. Many firms pay higher wages to the person working on odd shifts or days. The wages may be worth the inconvenience.

Disadvantages and Restraints

Odd schedule. It becomes difficult to adjust permanently to an odd schedule, because it will always be out of phase with the rest of the community. Therefore a regular routine of living may be difficult to establish.

Family disruption. The rest of the family, being on a more normal schedule, may find that adjusting to yours is disrupting. Planning times for church and school activities invites frustration. The family may lack unity and cohesiveness. This impact is greatest on the mother who must try to hold things together in the home.

Spiritual Dangers

Making excuses. With unusual working schedules, it becomes easy to excuse yourself from church, family, or spiritual activities. Don't allow your peculiar circumstances to keep you from what may be most needful in your life.

Withdrawing. Since your schedule is either undependable or different, it is easy to withdraw gradually from spiritual fellowship and from vital contact in your community. You must make special efforts to keep involved.

Having mentioned the few items common to these unusual jobs, let me offer some specific suggestions for each category.

The Shift Worker

Any shift other than the common eight-to-five places unusual pressures on you and your family. Your sleep schedule becomes confused, family activities are difficult to coordinate, and regular weekly involvement in any activity is almost impossible. Yet, taking practical steps to counter the problems and taking advantage of the schedule may change your whole attitude and perspective. I have worked shifts — the worst kind: my schedule was a ten-day cycle of two swing shifts, two midnight shifts, two day shifts, and then three and one-half days off. Some of these ideas helped me to adjust to that schedule:

Design your sleep schedule. Without adequate sleep, you cannot function properly. Your body has a built-in clock that is conditioned by habit, so you must help it adjust to your schedule. For swing shifts the change is not drastic: many persons function well on six or seven hours sleep with an occasional early afternoon nap and perhaps some extra weekend sleep. For the midnight-to-eight shift, the adjustment is more difficult, especially with a return to "normal" hours on the days off. Daytime sleep is probably best, though some function well on three hours before going to work and four or five in the morning after work. There is no easy adjustment for days off except to try to function on mixed sleep schedules with an occasional long (nine-to-ten-hour) period of sleep.

Do not expect the entire family to tiptoe around and be tense while you sleep. Have no phone in the bedroom. Use ear plugs for noise reduction: get specific ones made, if necessary. A fan or a similar constant noise in the room masks other sounds. Some like to have a well-insulated room in the basement. It is helpful to have a doorbell that can be disconnected.

Use daytime hours well. For doing projects, studying, or running errands, the daytime hours are better than evenings. You face fewer interruptions and can generally use a four-or-five-hour block. It is difficult to get even three consecutive hours in the evening. Chapter 7 explains how to use Saturdays. Your schedule will give the equivalent of two Saturdays. Apply the same ideas to your daily time off.

Adjust to weekends. It is critical to invest your days off in the family, since your presence during the week is greatly reduced. Try to flow with the family schedule rather than your own on weekends.

Give your wife a break. Your schedule will have almost as heavy an impact on your wife as on you. As you will be around more during the day, try to help her by caring for the children or doing specific tasks in the home. Don't make it seem that the whole world must adjust to your odd schedule.

Do not use your schedule as an excuse. Use your schedule to advantage in getting more done, not as an excuse for not doing certain things. When I taught at the Air Force Academy, I knew how full a cadet's schedule was. At the beginning I was awed by it, thinking that they really had very little time to be involved in spiritual activities. But I soon discovered that if a cadet *really* wanted to do something, somehow he found the time and opportunity. If he wanted to ski, he would end up on the slopes most weekends with various clubs and activities. If you really *want* to do something, you can and will find time and opportunity. You can find time for your family, your own spiritual growth, and an outreach to others — *if* you want to. If you don't want to, no amount of free time will make it convenient.

The Traveler

Regardless of the occupation, the person who travels a great deal faces special pressures and restrictions. I fit this category, for I am away from home about forty percent of the year. During certain shorter periods, the percentage may be higher. There are many things you can do to counter the problems raised in this kind of schedule. First let me note that many people travel even though they never leave town, that is, they are in so many evening and weekend activities that they might as well be gone. I too have made that mistake and had to come to grips with a hyperactive schedule.

Plan your travel. The further ahead you plan your travel, the better you and your family can adjust. But planning involves more than just scheduling in advance. Specifically I suggest that you —

— space your trips so that you are home more frequently;

— try to avoid traveling on weekends;

— don't plan many long trips in any given year; even if it costs more, make shorter trips;

— set a limit on the time you are gone;

— keep records of your "away" time; I count a day away by the number of evenings I am gone, because evenings are most important to my family;

— try to avoid last-minute changes;

— plan travel around key activities of your family and your local spiritual ministries;

— plan less travel during the summer months.

I wish to emphasize your being home on key occasions and important activities of the family. Basketball games, choir concerts, and birthdays are more important to your children than you might think. Your schedule will tell your children how important they are to you.

Guard your wife's role. When you are gone, a heavy burden falls on your wife. Financial decisions, child discipline, home maintenance, and myriad other things become her responsibility. The pressure can be devastating. If you do not plan carefully, she can step out of her biblical role. During the Vietnam conflict, servicemen regularly had one-year tours of duty overseas. Many marriages were destroyed as wives were forced to assume total responsibility for their families and grew to enjoy their independence.

Here are some ideas for helping your wife:

• Leave instructions where she can reach you on any given day.

• Plan with her how the children are to be disciplined. Inform the children that you will be in touch continually and will be involved in discipline decisions. This is more important as the children become teen-agers, since open rebellion and resistance tend to develop in the father's absence during those years.

• Enlist a friend or two to check on your family's needs in your absence.

• Make sure all your legal documents are in order in case of an emergency.

• Allow your wife financial freedom in your absence.

• Do not set standards for the children that your wife cannot enforce.

• Have a clear understanding of the kinds of situations in which she must call you.

Morality. Every person experiences moral temptations, but the traveler is especially susceptible. Time alone, motel rooms, and available pornography all contribute to this problem. There also is the insidious thought that because you are off where you are unknown, no one will know what you have done. One serviceman told me, "When you are ten thousand miles from home, you soon think you are ten thousand miles from God." Jealously guard your eyes, mind, and body in this matter. Live on the basis of the promises of 1 Corinthians 10:13. One helpful thing is to witness daily to someone — let others know that your reputation is aligned with God's standards.

Use time well on the road. When you travel you are away from customary commitments and often have extra free time. Plan constructive things to do: Bible study, Scripture memorization, correspondence. Accomplish things while traveling that will free your time once you return home. This will take planning for each trip. Also seek out Christian fellowship in the various places that you visit.

Take the children with you. Try to take each child with you once a year on a trip. You will have personal time with that child, and it will be an adventure for him. It will help him to understand some of the requirements of your work.

Use the phone. Call home frequently when you travel. Talk to your children, not only your wife. Your voice is the next best thing to your presence. You can handle many family decisions in this way. It *is* worth the cost. Your company may even allow this as a compensation for travel.

Special times with the family. When you travel a lot, special times with the family become even more important. Celebrating a birthday two days late *is* a problem to a seven-year-old. What *he* thinks is important is more crucial that what *you* think is important in his activities. Give special attention to vacations — make them family-centered.

Plan your time at home. When you are not traveling, try to spend extra time at home. Work shorter days if possible. Avoid traveling during school holidays or vacations. Remember that when you were gone, your wife carried an extra load; thus you should plan on easing hers when you are home.

The Seasonal Worker

Many jobs are seasonal in nature and require maximum effort for only part of the year. Typical examples are construction workers, farmers, school teachers, and harvesters. A common characteristic of these jobs is that a person may not work at all during part of the year and the amount worked is not totally sufficient to meet the financial needs of the family. Here are some practical suggestions to cope with this circumstance.

Prepare for the seasonal push. Realize that during the working season, you will be pushed for time and will have to work harder and longer. Prepare both yourself and the family for that adjustment by spending additional time with them during the off-season.

Discipline yourself financially. Seasonal variation means financial fluctuation. It is imperative that you save some money to carry you over the off-season time. Many seasonal jobs have a degree of insecurity of future employment. Therefore you need to avoid debt of any kind other than a home and medical needs.

Plan your off-season time. Depending on your financial needs, you must make definite plans for the off-season. Consider these ideas:

• Go to school or a training session to help you change your occupation to something more stable, or to make you more qualified in your present work.

• Develop off-season sources of income. This would be an opportunity to begin some kind of business or other self-employment.

• Give special consideration to your family, since they were likely neglected during your seasonal work push.

Stabilize your family. Family stability is extremely important. If it is necessary for you to change locations during your seasonal work or year by year, I suggest leaving the family in one place while you travel to the work location. Their stability is more important than your inconvenience for a short period.

Spiritual involvement and training. With extra time available, you have a good opportunity to devote time to your church or some community organization. It may give you the chance for some extensive spiritual training. Many churches, especially in larger cities, have special Bible training classes for laymen.

For many seasonal workers, a lack of education, job opportunity, and training imposes severe limitations for change. The earlier material in this book on adverse circumstances and on "pulling up roots" will be helpful to you. Never lose sight of the fact that God has placed you in direct contact with people in circumstances like your own for the purpose of sharing your faith with them.

NOTES

Chapter One

1. William Barclay, *Ethics in a Permissive Society* (New York: Harper and Row, 1971), p. 94.

Chapter Two

1. Howard Butt, *The Velvet Covered Brick* (New York: Harper and Row, 1973), p. 137.

Chapter Three

1. LeRoy Eims, *Winning Ways* (Wheaton, IL: Victor Books, 1974); and Paul Little, *How to Give Away Your Faith* (Downers Grove, IL: Inter-Varsity Press, 1966).
2. Walter A. Henrichsen, *Disciples Are Made — Not Born* (Wheaton, IL: Victor Books, 1974).

Chapter Four

1. Adam Smith, *The Money Game* (New York: Random House, 1967), p. 14.
2. Howard Butt, *The Velvet Covered Brick* (New York: Harper and Row, 1973), p. 125.
3. *Bits and Pieces* (Fairfield, NJ: The Economics Press, April 1975).

Chapter Five

1. Sara Welles, "When Your Husband's Out of Work and the Church Just Smiles," in *Eternity* (October 1974).
2. Ten Speed Press, Box 4310, Berkeley, CA 94704: available in paperback.
3. F. B. Meyer, source unknown.
4. J. Oswald Sanders, *A Spiritual Clinic* (Chicago: Moody Press, 1958), p. 183.

Chapter Eleven

1. *I Married You* (New York: Harper and Row, 1971); *Heaven Help the Home* (Wheaton, IL: Victor Books, 1974); *The Christian Family* (Minneapolis: Bethany Fellowship, 1970); *How to Be Happy Though Married* (Wheaton, IL: Tyndale House Publishers, 1968).

Chapter Twelve

1. Studs Terkel, *Working* (New York: Avon Books, 1975), p. 688.